G000144810

The True Dynamics
of
Life

The True Dynamics
of
Life

By
Mike Robinson

SOL Promotions Ltd 2010

The True Dynamics of Life

1st Edition 2010

Co-written with Jo Le-Rose

158. 1

Cover:
NASA: M104 Hubble Sombrero Galaxy
NASA: World
Collaboration Design by SR Print: www.srprint.co.uk

Edited and Typeset by SOL Promotions
Published by SOL Promotions

ISBN 978-0-9544478-5-4

iv

Dedication

Love is not a destination nor is there a path to reach it. It is something that breathes, moves and lives beyond the confines of human thinking. It has no levels, no systems and no labels and if you watch yourself with constant awareness, it may just breathe its bounty of treasure upon you, changing you for eternity.

You cannot reach love with your mind, because it is the unknown and your mind is only a machine built on your memories, your past and your beliefs. Love has none of these things in it. It is beyond the known. When you take away all what is not love, you are left with only love...

I dedicate this book to you. Underneath all you have become is the real you and it is this which is love, binding each and every one of us together as one.

Mike Robinson.

Contents

Part Two: Who Am I?

Acknowledgments

When you look into the heart of another, you will see your own reflection. Every moment upon my voyage of life has been filled with spiritual treasures and deep learning and I would like to thank all those that I have met along the way.

A special thank you also to:
Jo Le-Rose: this journey we have shared has been unbelievable and it just keeps unfolding. You have been there with me and for me every step of the way...Thankyou.
Cheyanne, Ian & Isla Lowther, Louiza Le-Rose: watching you all grow and spiritually mature these last few years has been my greatest joy.
Josie Jo, Ian, Cohen & Aiyanna Slater, Steve & Gabi Robinson: we can stand the test of time no matter what we go through.
Nigel Smith: you saw the truth and took action.
Sue Joseph, Mic McGregor & family: for giving the message a platform, and for your support and passion for life.
Sara Gibbons: for your relentless giving and willingness to seek only the truth.
Jennifer Stead: your patience, expertise and generous heart, has yet again proved to be invaluable.
Thankyou to those who have organised my workshops, one-day lectures and private sittings: Miriam Young, Sue Joseph, Madonna Sharpe, Anne Poole, Angela Pogson, Sue Thompson, Gwen Hanson, Tricia Hawkins, Jools Bond, Karen Wells, Jo Wynn and Christine Smit-Savory.
Hassan & Kalima Lazem: for your deep friendship.

Miriam Young, Nic Caine, Tracey Temple, Colette Evans, and Lisbeth Skovmand Nielsen: for your continuous support and friendship.

Arnaud, Lydie, Kloe & Astrid Ancely: the heart is stronger than any distance.

A huge thankyou to those who have attended workshops and residential courses over the last twenty years; we have been on a remarkable journey!

Finally, I have immense love and gratitude for that which is the very core of my life, and I am humble before its magnitude. Thankyou...

Foreword

Reading this book is like taking a cold shower: the shock takes your breath away. In that silent space lies the possibility of glimpsing a truth. You begin to realise it's doing something deeply disturbing to you.

Mike Robinson is one of those who have direct experience of that unitive truth which underlies all existence. That truth can only be felt, it cannot be captured in words; nevertheless, words are the only vehicles we have to describe it. Mike Robinson's words are idiosyncratic. His main focus is not as a writer, but as a speaker, a speaker with an urgent, compelling message, as thousands of people who have heard him will testify.

There is always some difficulty in reading transcriptions from recorded speech, since speech flows, and the speaker's intonation and gestures make the meaning clear. It's one thing listening to Mike speaking in a public space, and another thing reading his words on the page. Both are necessary. When you're listening, you wish you could have it in print in order to recall it, and when it's on the page, you wish for the author's voice, and his quiet but powerful physical-spiritual presence.

His advice to 'observe without judgment' in every moment applies to the activity of reading this book. As you read, you may realise you are judging it. But if you read on with an open mind, you may become aware that you are starting to become aware. What's more, as you read this or that sentence, you may be taken aback to find your nervous system resonating with the truth of it. This is reinforced when you do the exercises. You will get breakthrough insights into how you think, feel and act from moment to moment, and this revelation will prompt you to change the way you live your life, from one based on conditioning and fear to one based on openness and love.

Visionaries through the ages have warned people to reform. When they don't take heed, that society collapses because they're acting against the fundamental principles of the universe.

Enlightenment, awareness, is open to everyone who truly changes their perceptions. Mike Robinson's unique, visionary teaching is likely to open your eyes and your heart and lead you towards pure awareness, which is the only hope for ending the chaos in humanity.

J Stead.

Author's Note

Over the years I have had the privilege of meeting a great many people and I have been given the opportunity to discuss the enormous topic of life with them. Some of these people have lived their lives having a profound and intimate relationship with the truth, but others have refused to let the truth in, as they fear what it will do, so they have continued to hold onto their beliefs and opinions.

When I was a child, I had a belief that everyone saw, thought and felt the same way as I did, and it came as a shock to realise just how differently people think. I have since learnt how a person's ingrained conditioning, their religion, culture and fear is what separates them from another human being. It is this deep-rooted belief of separation that is passed down from generation to generation which has given me the passion to find out the truth for myself. The question I asked myself as a child was: If love is the one true emotion, how come we have become separate from each other?

For decades I have spoken about the suffering of humanity and the solution. Many people have come to listen and share, sometimes staying for one day, a weekend or perhaps even for a residential course. There have also been organised overseas trips to several countries with people from various cultures and backgrounds. Some of these people have taken the solution and applied it to their lives and others have not.

In 2002 my first book: The True Dynamics of Relationships was published, which was a guide to looking at all the relationships we have in life. This book was also a workbook and

5

I taught the principles of it globally, where it was fondly renamed by the participants as 'a kick in the pants'. In this book I made references to the subject of the soul and the many emotional layers of the human being, but what I have since realised, is how some people got stuck on the words. They could not get beyond the barrier of language and they wanted knowledge, facts, figures and details to store in their memory banks, and they were not discovering the truth for themselves.

It is far easier for a person to take the truth and add it to their current conditioned belief of the truth and do nothing with it. To drop the labels and the conditioning is too much of a difficult task for some, as they want to keep their false identity and stay in the pleasure and pain of their desires and dramas. This creates a conflict, because they are no longer going within to discover self-knowledge, as they are forming larger belief systems which take them even further away from the truth. The patterns which keep fear, pride, anger and jealousy active in their life still remain, and some people even continue to present themselves at the next workshop without having put self-observation into action.

This realisation of what the individual mind was doing caused me to deeply understand how you cannot take people to the truth. All you can do is point out the facts which are leading them into greater human suffering.

This book has therefore been written with this fundamental understanding of how truth cannot be given by using mere words. Only the illusion can be written about, as it is only by negating all that is not love, can love reveal itself.

You will not find any 'systems', 'isms' or 'path' in this book, but what you will find is a mirror, and only by self-observation, deep resonant realisation and action upon the truth, can you set yourself free, and therefore set the world free.

Mike Robinson.

Introduction

Most people are either too busy trying to become something other than what they already are, or they are trying to survive on minimal resources whilst dreaming of a better life. What is it that drives humans away from the peace of the moment? Is it our past memories, which are filled with fear from unfinished issues that continue to haunt us, or is it this constant reaching for an illusionary future? What is it *you* are using which keeps you caught in the past or running into the future? You are using your mind; you are thinking. It is your mind which moves into past memories and future dreams based upon your history and aspirations.

These past experiences, where you did not express yourself fully, or where you were made to feel worthless, are often the trigger points that the mind gets stuck on. To prevent these incidents from happening again, it creates mental scenarios of a future which does not include old fear patterns and issues, or it tries to justify its actions by replaying painful memories with a different outcome, but these actions are based on fear. All your memories are built on your experiences and each incident will have a like or dislike element to it. The mind wants to create more of its likes and less of its dislikes. Your memories of hurt and pain are the very pivot of your opinions, because your mind will think in terms of what you, or someone else, 'should' have done differently.

This striving to be free from the suffering, whilst still creating pleasurable experiences according to your desires, is what keeps you pre-occupied with future goals. Your mind wants you to be successful and live in the pleasure of that success. You may *think* there is nothing wrong with this, but it is a vast cycle of success versus failure. The current state of the world is proving that this mechanical pattern of constant movement between opposites does not work and is creating major world chaos.

There are very few people who want to be free of this machine and be who they really are, living beyond duality, chaos and suffering. Unfortunately, the majority are not aware of what is really going on and their ignorance, lack of self-worth and pain is what drives them to become someone else or be somewhere else. This very essence of being goal orientated and self-obsessed begins the process of the rat race, and once you start running and build up your momentum it will take a shock, a fall, or a brick wall to break your pace. Most shocks occur in the form of loss, from losing loved ones, loss of job, home, health, etc., but can you look at your life right now without having to be forced to do it by circumstance?

Only when you stop can you ask yourself what life is all about. Many people only question life, the Universe, God, etc., when things become problematic. When we are materially comfortable and there is plenty of everything and a feeling of being on top of the world, we say how great life is and we do not probe deeply enough into the recesses of our being. Yes, we may do charity work, or donate our unwanted things, but we do not really go inside and question exactly who we are. The second life throws us a challenge, or we are struggling to survive, we curse the heavens in despair and say, 'Why me?' Humans have this habit of only questioning the reason for living when their very existence is being challenged and when life is no longer fulfilling their desires.

When we do start to search for an answer to these problems we find many institutions and resources to turn to for help: religion, philosophies, new age, angels, gurus, psychics, etc. The variation is endless and we dabble in a bit of this and a bit of that, trying to find what appeases the appetite because it wants to 'know' the mystery of life. Maybe we become dazzled by some saviour who is supposedly there to help us, or we try to communicate with the invisible angels who are apparently floating around in the ether and protecting us. These belief systems give us a comfort zone and because we now feel spiritually safe, we stop probing further, but we are actually hindering our understanding of life, because belief, which is based on the history of the past, has stopped us from discovering the moment. We have become trapped by all the rituals, dogmas, chants, worship, etc., and these have covered over the space within us and it is this space which allows us to find out the truth. After a while of playing with these concepts, the old restless feelings start to emerge again and we find ourselves looking for the next guru or the next fix.

For generations someone external has described the workings of God and the Universe, but is it enough to believe the description of another's experience, or do you want to find out the truth for yourself? To know through another is a shoddy way of living and it only puts a plaster on a deep wound that needs cleansing and stitching. For example, the word 'soul' is spoken about so easily and the majority have heard of this word, but do you really know if the soul exists? It has been described in books, people have sung about it and some have even tried to paint it, but have you actually found it for yourself, or have you just accepted the general idea that we have a soul, which is a belief? To find out the truth for yourself sets you free, because then you are unshakeable.

Some people do not turn to any religion, philosophy, guru or psychic for an external solution, instead they remain locked in their suffering and may become insular, atheistic and cynical or they turn to some form of habit that reduces the pain of suffering, which can include alcohol, drugs, food, gossiping, shopping, etc. If you find yourself caught up in repeat habitual behaviour, you will need to acknowledge what you are running away from. These habits may help you to numb your erratic emotions and give you a false sense of relief, but once the 'high' disperses, you are left with the very issue which you are trying to avoid. This constant running away uses enormous amounts of your personal energy and you may often find yourself exhausted or ill. In reality, you are truly frightened, because there does not seem to be anywhere safe or anyone to turn to, so you live in this constant nervous fear and depression.

It is this very fear which prevents you from stopping and facing your life as it is, with all of its frustrations, anger, worries jealousies, etc. Fear keeps you running away from that profound sense of loneliness and the indescribable feeling of never being entirely heard or known by another. This vast void of not-knowing, which exists within the core part of your being, is what you are most afraid of, because when you enter into this space you will challenge everything you believe yourself to be.

This book is going to be your mirror, as it is going to confront you and bring forth any illusion, so that you can really look at it and see the truth for yourself. It is important to start with your life as it is right now, because you play a major part in society and ultimately the world. You need to be clear about how you have got to where you are today and where you have needlessly spent your energy. If you have been trapped by society, religion and your own thinking, which is built upon conditioning, then you will end this book knowing exactly who you are, why you are here and what you need to do.

Most of the content of this book will rub against your belief systems and appear to be controversial. You may even find yourself arguing points, attacking and defending, but this is just your conditioning reacting to the challenge. You have probably spent the majority of your life following ideals and the ways of society, but the very institutions which govern this world will need to be laid bare, so that you can see right through to their central intent and how you have been expected to play the game. Your own hidden agendas, your dependency on others, on society, and the ways you self-prostitute your spiritual essence will also reveal themselves. Once you have seen it clearly, you can let it go and heal all those parts of yourself which have been trapped by the illusion.

Nature is a major player on this planet, without it we will all die, so you will need to understand your relationship to it, and how it works, in order to purify it. You will see for yourself the forces that govern this planet and how each individual is being exploited by these forces and what you can do about it in your life. Nothing will be hidden from you any more and this is the greatest step to freedom. The real beauty is that I am not going to tell you, you are going to find out and realise it for yourself.

When you stop and observe something, free from the past and judgment, it reveals itself to you. This is the journey we are about to embark on. The second you judge, defend or attack what is written, then we have stopped the journey. You only need to read the words, observe the response from deep within yourself and listen for the truth behind the language.

Part One

Where Are We
Now As A Human Race?

Chapter 1

When is Enough, Enough?

The world is in chaos and that is a fact! If the world is in chaos, then each individual is also in a state of chaos, as we are intricately woven into the fabric of this world. In truth, we are consciously or unconsciously adding to this chaos in every moment, so at what point do we say, 'stop?'

See It As It Is.

What is the most important thing the world needs right now?
You have probably answered the above question with one of
the following: peace, love, joy, freedom or the end of all
suffering. I have put this question to thousands of people across
the world and the answer is always one of the above, therefore
there is a general consensus across the globe that the world
needs to change. People have had enough. As a race, the
human family has suffered for thousands of years and still we
have not reached a point where we can live in unity and peace.

Politics, religion and wealth have not answered the human
cry of desperation, as people are dying every day from famine,
disease and neglect. War is rife across the world, as is crime,
and we are besieged with contradictory beliefs and the
suffering we cause each other is astronomical. We have put our
faith and trust into politics, religion, etc., in order to better the
state of man, but still the endless bout of pain continues. Who is
going to help us? Who is going to sort out the mess we have
created? The sadness in the faces of those you pass in the street
is all too familiar, yet the blinkers that blind us to others keep us
focused on our own individual fight for survival. These blinkers
are what prevent us from globally asking, 'Why?' We need a
solution to the vast problem of human suffering, and we need it
now.

It is time for a complete overhaul, both individually and
worldwide, beginning with the word 'stop!' We need a moment
of stillness to reflect upon ourselves and the way in which we
live our lives. This is what this book is about. It is asking you to
no longer accept the old ways of working, which have created
chaos and madness, but to look at the underlying issue that
makes humans do what they do. There are three key questions
a person will ask themself at some point in their life.

1. Who am I?
2. What is it all about?
3. What is my life purpose?

Not knowing the answer to these three questions has brought about so much confusion and separation into the human family. These questions have been asked throughout the world and presented at the feet of the most important institutions of society and religion. The response has been conflictive and the answers are based on the beliefs according to what country you were born into and what religion you adhere to. Religion and the new age philosophy have mostly replied, 'You are spirit and you have come to evolve yourself into a God-like state and do good works in this world. If you do well according to the written words from a book, or from the guidance of the ascended masters, then you will be rewarded.' Society tells us, 'You have to be morally upstanding citizens, work hard, succeed and adhere to the laws set down by authority. You are no longer seen as individuals, but as a collective group.'

Is this all a big illusion? We have been following these ideas for thousands of years and we are still living in chaos. We need to find out the truth, because if we can look at something clearly, without opinion clouding our sight, we will see the folly behind it and the truth will surface. This act of stopping and observing will begin to transform chaos into order, but even though this is a simple solution, most humans cannot look at something without forming a judgment or an opinion. Our thoughts and actions have become habitual and most of us do not even realise we are doing it. We think it is normal to live a life of constant opinion and judgment and we have forgotten how to truly love.

How did we get to this Point of Chaos?

If we look back over the history of human existence we can see how we have always been at loggerheads with each other. The problems began in the home with the family unit, before expanding out into the community. For example, a husband and wife may have had a lack of communication due to unfulfilled desires and this would have affected those who existed around them. Even today, if we are honest, we will realise most of us

17

have a communication problem with our spouse, children and parents. Often, if the frustration which arises from this problem is not dealt with, we will find it extending outwards into the environment, where disputes with the neighbours may occur from issues of barking dogs, loud music, garden neglect, etc.

Before long, a whole village or town is having a communication problem and this creates an egregore, which is a ball of negatively charged energy in the air. A few miles away another village or town is doing the same thing and soon competition with each other begins through gang warfare, football teams, etc. Finally, our problems, which began in our own front room, find themselves extended into country waging war against country, all because we cannot communicate properly. Fundamentally, apart from technology, nothing has changed for thousands of years.

Another example of antagonism between humans is the creation of nationality. This is probably one of the most toxic illusions that humans have formed. People are often proud of their nationality and they boast about their country, but this pride is an act of separation, because you have just divided yourself from all others outside of your country and now there is a barrier to forming a healthy relationship with a supposed foreigner. For example, if you were a British soldier during the Second World War and you met a German soldier in the street, what would your reaction be? Even before you knew anything about the person, his likes, his dislikes, his history, the names of his children, etc., the fact that you are from warring countries would immediately make you enemies.

How can two people from different countries instantly hate each other on sight? Is it because both may have murdered people from the other's country? Who is responsible for this hatred, and how come we as individuals have accepted this way of life as 'normal'? Somewhere along the line we were told what to think and the argument was so plausible that we would even die or kill for it. If Hitler had ordered his men into Belgium, but all the soldiers turned around and said, 'No thanks mate', would there have been a war? Would Hitler have got on his horse as a one-man band and actually conquered Europe singlehandedly?

A human only has power over others if they give it to him by blindly following his orders. Each country has its own beliefs according to what is socially acceptable and people are spoon-fed these ideals from the moment they are born. We are conditioned by the dogmas of others and we do not even know it.

What exactly is this conditioning that teaches us the 'right and wrong' way to live? Has it been created by the government, religion, education, law, etc? Who keeps these institutions alive on this planet? The truth is, each one of us as an individual keeps these systems in place and we are responsible for the conditioning that we face in each and every moment. When a collection of like-minded individuals add their thoughts together it becomes what is known as a 'society'. It is this very creation which holds all the intellectual principles of the supposedly 'right' way to live. Human thought is therefore responsible for all the turmoil, because it is this which has created all the systems and the 'isms'.

Everything on this planet which is not a part of nature has been created by a mental concept: from our clothes, houses, vehicles, to methods of social control. In the very beginning, when humans first appeared on the Earth, there was only nature. There was no conditioning, no religion, no beliefs, no hierarchy, no governments, no money, no 'isms' and no systems. Through our interaction with nature we realised how some things brought pleasure, such as the smell of flowers, but other things would bring us pain, such as a bite from a snake, etc. In order to function we began to use memory to store our experiences based on the pleasure and pain they brought us, but we also began to psychologically worry about or fear those things which would bring us pain, so we became a part of mind, and desire formed, wanting the pleasure, but at the same time rejecting any pain.

The very fact that we can produce inspirational creations of art on the one hand, to weapons of mass destruction on the other, proves how the mind swings within its opposites of suffering and sublime. The problem lies not in the beauty we have produced, but in the pollution, the distortion and the pain we have created. Somewhere along the line we have lost our balance and we are not wielding the power of creation correctly. We have used our energy in ignorance, with catastrophic results.

The very first outpouring of human thought began the process of disorder. How can you relate this to yourself? Think of the person you like the least and look at that dislike. You will find underneath this intense feeling lies the root cause, and it is usually because the person is not doing things the way you believe they should be done. You have a belief and they are going against that belief. Now ask yourself where did this belief come from? Did it come from your ancestors, the law, religion, from your experience, etc.? Whatever answer you give will definitely be related to something you have learned from the past. Therefore, all thought is based on something from the past. The foundation of thought is memory. You cannot think without memory and this dislike of another is based on whether they bring you pleasure or pain. We see people as separate from ourselves and we are also taught to distrust those who hold beliefs which are different from the beliefs of the society that we adhere to.

This distrust creates irritation and antagonism, which often results in arguments, disputes and war. One issue, clearly highlighting this factor, is racism. How can the human, past and present, actually accept the belief that the colour of someone's skin denotes whether they should live, die, be subjected to poverty, be abused, be unworthy or be a slave. How can those who wield more physical or political power, annihilate human life, based on a decision of physical or racial difference? People have been murdered and subjected to horrific atrocities, all because the mind sees them as separate. The mind is the problem, not the race or the colour of the skin.

Each individual has this point of separation inside of themself. They see themself as different. Yes, genetically we

20

are, and also our own personal history gives us definition, but the basic principle for each human is the same. We all feel emotion, we all think and we are all living physical lives on this planet. Chaos begins in the individual mind, and this mind has been taught by other minds from birth on how to be separate. It is the greatest disease, which is being passed on from generation to generation, and still it continues.

What Gives Chaos its Power?

Thought itself is a learnt commodity. From a very young age you were taught the language of the country you were born into and you learnt the descriptive names for every item you looked at. You communicated with others through sound, but if there were no language how would you think and communicate? Would there still be chaos?

Thought is a tool used to describe the familiar. The second an item is labelled it stops being something to discover. For example, you look at a flower and immediately your mind recognises it from memory and says, 'That is a rose.' The label has become more important than the observation of the colour, the light on the petals, etc. If you are able to see the descriptive tools for what they are, drop them and go back to observing life, then you are not being governed by the mind. Problems occur when the mind takes over and all that is significant to the person is mind-based knowledge.

People are often gauged on their ability to memorise information and the whole educational system is built on this capacity to hold information. This is what will give you a university degree, but it is just knowledge based on descriptive language. It is empty and only useful for intellectual pursuits. By the time you finish your education you will have spent nearly a quarter of your life training your memory, and you will spend the next twenty or more years climbing the ranks at work, only to find out that when you die descriptive knowledge is of no use whatsoever.

If knowledge is only meant as an aid for living, then what has happened? Surely labelling something cannot cause the deep-rooted chaos which is prevalent on this planet. Is there something else affecting the thinking process, and if so, how is it creating this distortion? Love can only create love, so was mind created by love? Where did it come from, and is there anything beyond the mind? These are deep and probing questions which need to be looked at if you are to understand yourself.

Each individual is responsible for their own thought world and it starts from the moment you wake up. How many times do you get out of bed, fall into the bathroom, look into the mirror and immediately think a negative thought about yourself? In this single moment you have just put more violence, anger and distortion into the world and you have not even left the house for work! This is an act of self-judgment, which is opinion. Even positive thoughts are still a judgment because they are in relation to an opposite. They are created by the mind, which is subconsciously seeking self-fulfilment by pleasurable pursuits whilst resisting and blocking pain.

This movement of the mind between the two opposing forces is fed by desire, which is emotional in nature. According to what you look at, the impulse to strive for it, or reject it, will be based on the pleasure or pain that you feel. The desire to seek success, to have material possessions, to be acknowledged and known, to have power over others, to win wars, to have direct access to God and all the rest of the things we do in order to 'obtain', are controlled by your feelings of like and dislike, which are your memories from the past, put into action in the present. If we are caught in these opinions, then nothing new can be found in the moment because it is filled with the past and future goals.

Each dualistic thought you have, which is born from this root of pleasure and pain, attracts similar thoughts to itself from others. For example, if you think negatively about the prime minister, then your energy actually moves into his space and deposits your thoughts. If there are similar thoughts of dislike already there, then they mingle together to create a dark, destructive egregore and this begins to expand out, filling the ether with damaging thoughts.

Millions of like-minded thoughts collect together every second and the energy is alive and autonomous. It is a force to be reckoned with. This energy has one purpose which is to accomplish what the original intent of the thought was, so if you feel that the prime minister should resign and there are millions agreeing, then before long it will be accomplished. These invisible forces are around us all the time, affecting our every move. This is why the presence of some people makes us feel positive and light and that of others makes us feel dark and moody. Their whole energy is being affected by their thoughts of others and themselves, and the thought projections from others, and we are either consciously or subconsciously aware of the state of their energy.

The ether of this planet has been polluted by the thoughts of humanity and this effect can be seen in the turbulence of nature. Global warming is accelerating due to the greed of man: the mass producing for consumerism, domestic and commercial waste, excessive mining, carbon monoxide gases, destruction of the rain forest and so forth. Behind every one of these lies the thought of man who is solely accountable for the slow annihilation of this planet. Therefore each and every one of us is responsible for keeping corruption existent upon this planet. Every single thought that you have is a potential toxic hazard and only you can regulate what you think.

What are we Really Searching For?

What are we really crying out for? Is it for more money, better health, food, shelter, etc.? Are we asking an external authority to give it to us? Are we blaming and condemning ourselves and others for our situation? Or is there some deep fundamental cry which goes beyond this material life? Have we had enough of the emptiness that living through suffering brings? Is the cry for something that no-one or nothing external can supply? Is there a deep sense of loneliness inside of you where ultimately you are lost and you do not know how to be and how to live?

Does this feeling of absolute loneliness or emptiness follow you everywhere? Is there an understanding that no-one really knows you or sees you for who you are and relationships always seem to be pretentious or somehow lacking? Does the meaning of life seem to elude you and can no-one answer this vital question which has no words? If you feel this, then you have the essential catalyst for a breakthrough. This constant essence of restlessness is the very thing which will catapult you into questioning the absolute basis of your life. There is only one true question that burns inside of you and there is only one answer, and you will need to explore both in depth in order for you to come into your own inner core, realise the truth and know exactly who you are.

We have suffered as a human race, we are separated individually and globally and we have seen how we are in serious need of a turn around if humanity is to survive much longer. There needs to be a change, as the old ways of doing things are not working. Mind and thought play a huge part in the way this world works. Their core dualistic nature, based on pleasure and pain, is detrimental to the existence of life on this planet.

The human being is crying for release, so what would it take for us to all start again? We cannot expect this of others; we can only ask it from ourselves. The question is, do we really want it? Is the passion for the truth deep enough? It is said that we only learn through suffering, but this statement is a lie, because we as a human race have suffered for thousands of years and still we have learnt nothing.

Chapter 2

Does Society Really Care?

We form conflicting opinions, perhaps about our parents, children, brothers, sisters, politicians or the woman next door, etc. These little conflicts play out in our thoughts as images and we discuss them with other like-minded people who agree with and reinforce our statements. But these little conflicts are just energy, negative distorted energy, which the mind sends out and affects those whom we have a problem with. Maybe these people are already having a hard time and have now got a little bit more suffering to endure, because we have sent them our reinforced negative beliefs. These beliefs have nothing to do with them, but they have everything to do with us. This is the responsibility of life, to know exactly how we affect others, and consequently, the world.

What is Society?

Society is made up from a collection of human thought. The early forms of society were groups of people who banded together and worked out the best way of living. The daily work of crop growing, hunting and child rearing was divided between the people in order to survive and progress. Language then developed, followed by the written word and these ways were passed from generation to generation, who also added further rules for an acceptable way of living.

Problems began at the same time as this early form of society was being created because the desire for more started to creep in. Even the very first group hunt would have showed the signs of desire. Maybe the one who killed the animal was raised up as triumphant and given praise by others in the village, but the ones who laboured over the washing of the clothes at the river were perhaps not noticed, so people began to see how certain tasks were more pleasing to the village than others. The feeling of wanting to be labelled as good and worthy and be acknowledged would have created a sense of competition and so envy was born.

From the thoughts of competition and envy came the very foundation of the continuous wheel of pleasure and pain. We desire all the good things in life and we reject all the bad things. Society is trying to build up a system which includes only the good. It is trying to live in one side of duality, i.e. the white side. At the opposite end of the spectrum is the black area and if we do acts of bad behaviour we are punished and sent to a dark place called prison, and we are no longer allowed to live in society. Hopefully, over a period of time, we will be re-educated to be good, so that we can once again join the ranks of social respectability.

The problem with pleasure and pain, or the spectrum of white and black, is that they are symbiotic, where one is the other will soon follow. For example: I see a bright red Ferrari and messages of pleasure are sent to my brain through the eyes and I say, 'Wow, I want one of those.' The mind quickly responds to the pleasurable impulses and I get future images of myself driving the car and I feel how jealous or proud other people will be of me. The desire for the Ferrari has begun, and to fulfil my desire I fight for a promotion and work more hours in order to make the money to buy the car. After six months the stress begins to show, as my health starts to deteriorate and my relationship with my family suffers. In the end, I have moved from the pleasure and into the pain, which has come about from my original desire.

The same can be said for pain. How many times have you gone through a painful experience only to say, 'I needed that to happen because I got something better out of it'? Or have you ever said, 'Well, we are at rock bottom, so the only way is up'? So, even in dire circumstances, pleasure also follows painful experiences.

The mind cannot function only in the good, because desire and the drive to be known and recognised are too prevalent in the human psyche. Society is therefore a mind-made system and no matter how it tries to incorporate only pleasure, pain will always be just behind it, following it in.

The Walls of Society

Let's go back to the hunter who killed the animal. Maybe when he arrived back in the village to feed the community he was celebrated, and after many more hunts he has now become an expert on the ways of hunting. People look up to him and seek him out for advice. Some of the villagers decide he should look after the whole village and make decisions which will benefit everyone. Other people, who do different tasks, which are maybe not recognised as important, disagree, and the village becomes divided, so a vote takes place. The hunter is voted in by the majority and he appoints his friend as his helper.

Authority and hierarchy are now taking shape and before long people stop listening to their inner knowing and follow the instructions of the hunter. His sons are born and they too are proven to be good hunters, so they take his place upon his death and his daughters are married only to worthy hunters, who hope their children will have the great hunter in them.

Generations later, we have more people and a council is created, laws and rules are set and the hunters also form a group to protect the community from invading animals or other tribes. As the community grows so does power, authority, wealth, trade and hierarchy, until we reach where we are today, which also includes nations, governments, wars, poverty and starvation.

What started off as a small band of like-minded people has expanded out into huge egregores of vast churning machines, which want to build more power and more wealth. Each country has its own society, its own way of doing things. If one country believes another country should change its way of doing things, or wants its fertile lands for its own, it declares war and millions of people are sent out to massacre other humans who have been deemed as separate from them.

For generations this way of killing has been accepted and we think nothing of training eighteen-year-old youths in combat systems. After an acceptable amount of time in preparation they are sent by the government to war-torn areas to butcher other people's sons, daughters, fathers, brothers, mothers and sisters, and we call it a fight against terrorism, or a necessary war for national security. We even give people medals and recognition for their war efforts, but when a crime occurs in the slums of a city, involving the stabbing of young kids by opposite gang warfare, we cry in outrage and demand justice. Is this not a reflection of war on a smaller scale? Or does it become a 'crime' because neither side is backed by a government? In some countries children as young as ten are taught the basis of war and given weapons with the intent to kill. Is this the future that our children can look forward to?

How can we be so contradictory? How can we wage campaigns in schools against bullying and punish children for hitting other children, yet when they get to eighteen we send them off to train as legal murderers? The military and the police force have often been found guilty of bullying and if these very same institutions are what we created to protect society, what does this say about the workings of society? It is a system that separates, divides and contradicts. It works for its own needs and betterment in the areas of power and wealth and it has a dynamic ability to control and manipulate the masses. There are two groups in any society, those that have, and those that do not have, and there is a wall between them.

This separation can also be seen globally. On a recent trip to a collection of eighty-three islands in the Pacific called Vanuatu, we were blessed to meet people who live very simple and mostly tribal lives. Cooke originally found the islands and stayed there for a while, calling it the New Hebrides, and in the nineteen-seventies the local people re-named it Vanuatu, which means the lands before time. After Cooke left it was rifled by pirates who found nothing to take, but in their greed they massacred thousands of simple people who had no weapons. On the islands there are no predators, no snakes and nothing poisonous.

The only other external force to have made an impact on them was Christianity, and on the main island of Efate, which has a 140km circumference, the major segments of Christianity have taken hold and separated the people. The clash between old tribal beliefs and religion has led to a lot of confusion and frustration about how they are supposed to live their lives and this has created forms of domestic abuse.

The islands themselves have no material value in that there is no gold, precious stones or oil to be found there. The only thing it has is the most incredibly rich fertile soil. Hence, it was found to be unimportant to other wealth-seeking countries and it was left alone. The technological age has therefore virtually by-passed Vanuatu. Even now, the tribal people marvel at the invention of the car and the mobile phone!

Recently, it is being exploited by land-seeking people and they are buying the land very cheaply from the tribes and building villas and expensive hotels. Very few of the tribes work with or understand money issues, as theirs is a sharing and trade way of life. Money is a new concept to them and they do not have such things as taxes or VAT, so business entrepreneurs are using them for capitalisation and cheap labour and they are making a lot of money along the way.

I am using Vanuatu as an example of what we do to those who are naive and simple. We are such a greedy race that we would take something so innocent and violate it in order to get more wealth and power. On just one of their tiny islands, we have murdered their people, used them, manipulated them, taken them away from nature into rituals and dogma, deceived them and now we are taking their lands. To just sit and watch these people work the land and fish has more value in the learning of humility, and we thought we were educating them...

This is what the human is capable of when its desire is strong. It separates itself from another and then proceeds to manipulate it to get what it wants. The very wall between one human and another is desire, and from this point thoughts of envy and competition seep into the goodness of the human heart, until only a selfish, empty shell remains.

Is having any Government Beneficial to the Human Race?

Society is a man-made system and every country is governed by an organisation which contains hierarchy, authority, rules, wealth and power. These so-called authorities determine the life of every individual and we vote them in to be of service to the betterment of humanity, but corruption is rife and suffering has become a normal way of life. There are millions across the globe homeless or without funds to feed their families. In countries such as Africa very few of the donated funds actually find their way to the people, as backhanders are common and greedy officials take for themselves and leave their people without any hope. Egypt has virtually become a police state where officials bully others, even those who have absolutely nothing, for bribes and payments, and they do it in the name of 'baksheesh', which means to share your wealth. Some people in India maim their children for sympathy begging, thousands are starving, and many are suffering from severe outbursts of malaria. There are problems in China as the rice crop fails, bringing famine and economic problems. Worldwide, single parent families suffer in absolute poverty with no way out. They are told to get an education, but it costs the one commodity they do not have: money.

The world system at present is not working. It is time to stop and really look at what it means to be a human being on this planet. Obviously it is not enough for us to see the death, the decay and the destruction we cause each other. As long as we are OK and it is not happening in our own back yard, then we can turn a blind eye to all the fuss. We have now come to the point of human evolution where we must ask if we should continue in the same vein of selfish acts and world destruction, or do we, as individuals, take charge of our lives and begin the process of change?

In order to change something we have to accept it in its current state. We have to observe the government and understand what exactly is holding the system together. Under all the rules and dogma you will find the initial intent and this is held in place by the general public's belief systems. When you look closer, you will see the hierarchy at play.

There are those who are really unfortunate, who have no food and basic living amenities, and there are those who may have enough for basic living, but they are trapped in poverty and possibly unclean living conditions. Others seem to be on a middle ground and have enough to keep things in balance, but the grind of daily life is likened to a machine, one step back and you could find yourself in the 'unfortunate' pile, so you become a slave to society. Above the middle ground is a more comfortable level where you are stable and you are holding a powerful role in society. The mega powerful people above these hold the keys to the government and have a large say in the running of the country, and finally, there are those very few who are super-powerful and everyone below them are like puppets on a string.

This is the basic ladder of society, but how did the unfortunate end up in such dire circumstances and why is the gap between the superpowers and the needy so vast? Is it all about power? Or is it just a monetary issue? How can we solve this problem which was created by the human mind as a model for living? Some people may argue that those who are wealthy have rightly earned their money. This may be correct, as some make their wealth through business, but who are their clients? Everyone needs clothes, food, homes, water, heating, etc. Some of the wealthiest companies supply these products and if you have no money, tough, go without. Most of those in poverty cannot afford the products that are mass-marketed today, nor can they afford a university education or a military commission to get further up the ladder. There is no way out for some, all because of the circumstance they were born into, which was created by humans themselves.

We have to stop and accept the responsibility for global starvation, the water shortages, the mass pollution, the mass waste and the complete separation from each other. We are totally out of balance and fallible and the government as a whole is too far removed from those at the bottom who are dying from the carnage of disease and famine. If there was such a thing as unity of man would you allow anyone to die from lack of food or clean water? Would the prime minister or president of that country allow his own child to die this way? Would he allow his daughter to be sold into prostitution and his son to get caught up in gang warfare? Anyone with love in their heart would not have this happen to their children, so why do we allow it to happen to others? What in the system is not working? Let's be honest. What is the fundamental reason why we, as individuals and as a society, allow another human being to suffer? What do we get out of it? What is the pay-off?

Even ploughing huge amounts of money from taxes into the system has not solved it. Money is therefore not the solution. What does the government really get out of society, from the members of parliament right through to town councillors? Is it power they are after? Is the real issue down to a simple model of hierarchy, i.e. I am above and they are below, so I can control it? Some countries don't even get the choice to vote for those who govern them. They are stuck with a dictator and they are mass controlled by one human being. How can we let this happen? This is the situation we are presently at within the human psyche: we allow ourselves and others to be abused.

If we could stop and drop all that is not working and start again would we put a different way of living in place? What would the new way involve? It would be pointless just dealing with one country because the problem is global, so you would have to work on the world as a whole. There are three major aspects on this planet, humans, environment and nature, and each one of these needs a serious amount of healing because humans have worked against the natural flow of things. We have created vast pollution with our current way of being, so the environment would have to be purified in line with the laws of nature and all atrocities to nature would have to be stopped.

Basic living and hygiene should be a right for every human, as should food, shelter and healthcare. At this point would money be needed? If you saw the other person as yourself would you help him? Would money be an issue? The only thing that separates you and another human being is your thinking and what you believe in. The mind cannot solve the problem, because it only thinks in terms of pleasure and pain, and love is not related to either term. What we need to do is negate what is not love. Anger, comparison, competition, jealousy, pride, envy, etc., are not the works of love, so what is left? We have honesty, compassion and pure acts, which have no intent or motive behind them.

For deep healing to take place in these three aspects, every single human would have to drop their conditioning and let go of their belief systems. There would be no separate nationality; you would be one individual in the total human family. This planet does not belong to anyone; it is for all of us to live here. To separate it into segments and have a war with another segment because they do things differently is ludicrous.

Can the world at present drop everything to become one? Or would people still hold onto their customs, their religions, their power and their wealth, because it is these divisions that keeps society working in the same vein as it always has.

Education would need a complete overhaul, as the present system of filling you with pointless information, is killing spiritual creativity, which is needed to develop honesty, compassion and pure acts in order to heal nature. The education of life is more important than learning about the 'great wars'. In the observation of one flower you will find mathematical equations, biology, geography, botany, herbalism, medicine, history and most important of all, its spiritual essence. Education about the meaning of relationships is also crucial to a child's growth and balance in the world. In one relationship you will find all the emotions which need to be worked on. In two lessons alone we now have a foundation for relating and understanding nature, but education is currently far removed from this. We are turning out mentally-trained adults who have no idea about their emotional state or the inner workings of nature, yet they are our hope for the next generation?

Another crucial issue to tackle would be the Governments, as they would have to drop their separate parties and end their bickering. A party leader fights only for the group's beliefs, yet they state how they are here to help all people. No, they are here to help *some* people. It is an elitist act. The whole workings of the government have been built on division, arguing, greed opposition, deceit and corruption, yet still the public vote them in. Why? If there was an election and no-one voted, what would happen? What if the public joined together and said, 'No' to the government, what would happen? The government exists because we let it and it starts with each individual.

If you began to look within yourself, saw all of your beliefs and conditioning and immediately dropped them, would it alter the whole of your life? Would those around you still have power over you? What if everyone in your whole village, town or city did the same thing at the same time? It would have a knock-on effect, and before long, the whole country would be dropping its illusions, its striving, its wealth issues, power and hierarchy.

This is the inner revolution and the outer will always follow the movement of the inner. It only takes one person to affect their family, the village, the country and ultimately the world. We do not need a government, we just to need to be who we really are and live life with spiritual intelligence.

Does Society Benefit You?

Society can be likened to a slug. Each one of us is in this slow moving slug. If we continue to add to the slug of society through being a good citizen, being in employment, paying our taxes, pensions, insurances and creating successful ventures, then the slug will carry us. The second an experience in life causes us to stop, such as childbirth, death, burglary, unemployment, old age, single-parent status, etc., we are thrown out of the slug and on to the slimy sidelines. At this point we have to take something from society, for instance, benefits, insurance, maternity time, etc., and we are now a liability to society. If we can take very little time to adjust and get straight back into society and back into the slug and give once more to this vast drudgery, then we are again embraced. If, on the other hand, our situation grows more difficult, i.e. we cannot find employment, or we cannot find child-minding facilities, then society starts to dispose of us. This may mean living on the poverty line and moving into a serious state of despair. Whilst we are adding to the benefits of society we are supported, but once we stop, we are disregarded and penalised.

There are also those who are parasitically feeding off the slug. They take when they are fully capable of work or of giving back to the community. They are not socially educated from the beginning about life and so they follow the belief patterns of those around them. Boredom in the mind can lead a person into drugs and crime. A lack of self-worth can also do the same, but the whole of humanity is responsible. We all created it and we all keep society alive by feeding it and somehow we all feel helpless to change it.

35

The mind is trying to find a solution to the mind. Is that possible? Have you ever looked at how your mind argues with you? For example, you see a delicious cake and your mind says, 'Go on have a slice', so you eat it. Within minutes of enjoying the pleasure of it, your mind now says, 'Oh no, now I am going to get fat!' The same mind told you to eat it and then the same mind berated you for eating it! How can something which has created so much contradiction on this planet put it right? If it attempts to rectify its own negative works, will the minds of those who hold the power on this Earth try to come against the solution? Will those, who make huge profits from the desolation of humanity, really want to change?

Is there a way for humans to live together without the cruelty of governments, religion, hierarchy, society, war, famine, murder, etc? Why did we create it all in the first place? Is it because the basic underlying nature of humanity has a distortion in it, or is it because the mind has become autonomous? Is the mind no longer a tool for discovery, but an entity that is only concerned with its own survival? These are the questions we want answered. We need to find out the truth because the illusion is killing us.

We asked if society really cares. Society is based on the whole loop of pleasure and pain, so it cares as long as you play the game of giving it what it wants. If you need, then the giving is very minimal and if you take without need, you will be punished. It is a huge entity which has no real interest in you and your life. You are in service to it and if you are not, then it will reject you. It is a mind-made system which lacks honesty, pure acts and compassion.

Even those institutions which are supposedly doing 'good' in the world have an underlying intent. For example, is there a sense of achievement in bringing good to another? Is there an exchange or pay back, or is it possible to do something without any attachment or intention? Where there is intent, there is thought behind it and thought is the reason why there is so much chaos on this planet. A real society, which exists without the constant striving, and lives beyond the traps of the mind and its dual aspects, cannot be built on any human separation and hierarchical authority. If your good works are built on hidden feelings of being better off than those whom you give to, then your giving has very little worth. Really question why you give to charities or fight causes. What is your hidden intent?

Chapter 3

The Human Conditioning

Get to know yourself for who you are, because the key to freedom is self-knowledge. It begins from the moment you are born. Do not let the world fill you up with its garbage and its expectations of you. The inner revolution does not cause you to implode; it makes you explode from the inside out. Nobody can give it to you, you have to find it for yourself, and self-knowledge is what will set you free.

What Exactly is Conditioning?

The mind itself is built from memory. It is a data-collecting instrument that relies on past experiences for information on how to deal with the present moment. When an event occurs, the mind has the ability to assess the situation and take out of its memory banks the tools needed to solve the equation, but when a completely new experience arises, where the mind has no past knowledge of how to react, a tiny window opens and there is a moment of stillness from within. Some people have described this stillness as shock, or peace. This very small window is where the past meets the present and is able to create the future.

Memory, or your past history, is the 'known experience' and the present moment is the 'unknown experience'. At this point of 'space' not only does memory assess and analyze, but there is also the intuitive feeling zone of fight or flight, i.e. face it or move away from it. Now you have the mind and an intuitive gut feeling giving you information on how to act, but there is one more element that also demands a response from you, and that is fear.

For example, you meet a snake on the path. Instantly your mind describes what it sees and says, 'That is a snake.' Your gut feeling will tell you to either move away because the snake is dangerous, or walk forward, as the snake is harmless, but fear would make you question your actions and override your impulse. This creates non-action and your thoughts and emotions begin to throw up all the learnt mental chatter of 'what if' and feelings of doubt, worry and hesitation begin to surface.

Most people are making daily decisions and living from this point of fear and they are caught up in a confused way of dealing with life. You may say the solution is for people to act on their intuition, but most people do not know how to hear their own inner voice, because it has been covered over with something else and they have lost the ability to listen. We have been taught to rely on external authority and dismiss the inner impulses. How did this occur and why do we accept it?

You, and everyone else, on this planet have been programmed with various belief systems and these have been taught to you from birth through the use of language. Mind has been trained over generations to rely solely on language to communicate and it has become very powerful, whereby people often control and dominate others by using the mind. If you look at all the rituals in religion and philosophy, they have been passed down through language, either verbal or written. Language itself is actually built on the opposites of right and wrong. Every fairytale story has good and bad in it, so does every novel, newspaper, magazine, TV programme, etc. All judgments are based on what we believe is acceptable or non-acceptable behaviour according to the society we live in.

When we really look at language we can see how the label itself has absolutely nothing to do with what it is describing. For example, the word 'tree' has no relationship to the actual living entity that exists behind the word. When you take away the label and observe the tree something else happens. Observation is an act without the mind interrupting it with all of your past learnt knowledge. So what in you is now experiencing this living entity? It is sensation or feeling. Beyond the labels of the mind lives a world of sensing. You may have been taught words, but who taught you how to feel?

When you are born you are an empty vessel. You have no memory and no thinking ability in terms of language. You think by feeling. As you grow older your parents or carers instil in you their beliefs about what is right or wrong, so your way of acting and perceiving on this planet is being shaped from your very environment. For example, your Uncle John comes to stay and you have a gut feeling that there is something dangerous about this person, but your parents tell you to stop being silly, as everything is OK, because this is a member of your family and this makes your Uncle John a safe person. They have overridden your feeling with language and labels and now you cannot trust your feelings any more. From this point on you rely on the external to tell you what is right or wrong for you and you become fearful. The intuition is able to relay the truth of any given situation, but each time you ignore your feelings you move further away from it.

Fear is therefore formed in a grey space between the mental label and your gut feeling. It is the sum total of your conditioning, which is your memory, and it is the axis for the movement between pleasure and pain. For example, if you had no memory of snakes and you had never been told about them, what would you need to trust if you came across one? It would be your gut instinct, and you would feel the snake and instantly understand its way of being and its intent in that moment. There would be no memory to give you mental chatter of all the learnt information about snakes and you would be able to act accordingly without any fear.

If your memory holds taught beliefs that snakes are dangerous predators, then the second you see one, you would react by trying to reject the possible outcome of pain. At this point you would begin to play mental scenarios and your emotions would be thrown into a panic. Your intuition would not be heard and you would take inappropriate action. This battle between mind, intuition and fear is what every individual faces in every moment.

Memory is the Past

Every thought you have is from the past. Thought does not exist in the moment, because the moment itself is the unknown and past is the known. When you bring the past into the present you destroy the moment, because now there is nothing new to discover and everything has become familiar. For example, you see a multi-coloured bird on the tree outside and you start to observe it. Before long, your mind brings forward the name of the bird and all of its habits and history and you begin to recall the last time you saw this type of bird, etc. You have now come out of the moment and you are on a journey in your memory, which is linked to past experiences.

You cannot think about anything new, because as soon as a thought arises it becomes memory and moves into the past. Right in this moment can you think of anything new with your mind? Even if you think of an ugly monster, somewhere in its features it will have what has already been thought about, for instance, maybe it will have one eye and a set of claws, etc. All these things are not new, as they are from your memory and mind was built to store memory, in order to understand nature and the environment. It was not formed in order to control you, take you over and govern your life.

Is it possible to live in the moment without the past? You need memory to be able to function in a chronological way, such as remembering your way home, how to do your job etc., but do you need the past as a fear-based, emotional and psychological machine, that is, do you need to keep thinking about your hurts, your fears and all the instances of 'what if' and 'what should be'? Or is the drama what you actually like? Is there a pay-off to having these pains? Does it make you feel alive and are you addicted to the emotions?

When you were born the first label given to you by your parents was your name. Since then you have either being given, or shaped for yourself, a mixture of positive and negative labels. You will have a personality based on likes and dislikes, your strengths and weaknesses, and you may also have a job title, a nick-name from friends, be a mother, father, etc. All these titles which have been created by yourself and others form many little images of you, and each mini you will be required to act differently according to who you are with. This is fragmenting the self. There are now many different parts of you playing various roles, and this is why there is division and separation in the world, because there is division and separation in each individual.

If you take away your labels, i.e. your name, gender, nationality, the religion you follow, the government party you vote for, any family titles you have and your job description, what is left? When you die at the end of this life you will have to let go of everything. Can you psychologically let go of everything whilst you are still alive? Letting go of the false you does not mean you give up your life and become monastic. It means to let go of the attachments to all your labels, your desires, your striving, your envy, etc., and see yourself as you really are. Look at your life as it truly is and not how you want it to be. When you are not being all these things, who exactly are you?

We are always striving for an end result. Is it possible to be with the journey moment-to-moment rather than always having your thoughts, which is your energy, focused on something far away? The very act of stopping and seeing life as it truly is will bring you into the moment. The second you begin observing your mind all the memories which have been stored within will begin to come forward. This is a great step to freedom. If you do not get caught up in the memory and just watch it, you will see it flow into your awareness and out again. Fears, which live in your mind through your memories and your conditioning, have been governing your life from a very young age. Is it possible to see this, realise it and take action to live beyond it?

Is there a Life Beyond the Mind?

We are all searching for something whether we are conscious of it or not. We are trying to find the one thing which will give us the freedom and the peace that we crave. We search for it in so many ways, through knowledge, religion, techniques, rituals, meditation and physical pursuits. We also look to others to tell us the 'way' and we get disappointed if they fail to live up to our expectations, or we beat ourselves up if we do not succeed to live up to another's idea of what we 'should be'.

The mind is always seeking something. It is always trying to become something other than what it is. If you were to really look at your life you will see how right from the beginning you were groomed to become 'something' or 'someone'. Your parents began the process, closely followed by education and society. Everyone expects something from you and you begin to move further and further away from who you really are into a moulded version, which may cause you to get exasperated, because no-one seems to know the real you and very few people are willing to scratch beneath the very cleverly-polished veneer of your label or your image.

Everyone is doing it. Everyone has a label or an image which they present to the world and your images are built from your learnt conditioning, from your mind which thinks in words, language and descriptive patterns. Underneath all of this is there anything 'real' in you? You may say you have good morals, that you are kind, generous, determined and strong, but what are all these words? They are descriptive labels created through beliefs from your past experiences. They describe an outcome. For example, if you are in an abusive relationship and you are 'strong' enough to get out of it, what was it that led you into it in the first place? The outcome was strength, but what was the real reason behind the situation?

We are asking if there is something inside of you which has not been touched by the mind or by beliefs and conditioning. Is there something beyond all of this, or are we born just to be filled up with language, habits and patterns in order to die? What would be the point in that? Or are we afraid to truly live as our real self, letting ourself become complacent with just a description of life and following that description, calling it law, order, society etc.? We live second-hand lives because we conform to the rules around us and we accept all that is told to us. We have become trapped by these rules and we deny ourself the freedom to enquire and find out for ourself.

This second-hand living is the very basis of society and religion. Three hundred pages could be written on how to get to God and what you will experience, see and feel, but at the end of those three hundred pages what has actually taken place? You have been fed with a descriptive account which has no bearing on the truth at all. The point is to always question. Look within at everything which is being said to you; go beyond the descriptive mind and all of your conditioning to see if there is something beyond what has been taught to you from the external. Real discovery of the self occurs in the space beyond words, where you can see something in its entirety.

The understanding is instantaneous and all of the components and its effect in your life are revealed. This 'space', which allows you to see the truth, is what you are really looking for.

Conscious Verses the Unconscious

We may say that we do not know we are conditioned and we may describe how we are trying to live a good life by doing the best that we can, but who or what is this best according to? What are we gauging our actions on? If someone tells you how well you have done, does this mean you have done well according to their expectations and beliefs? Look at your life. Look at the house you live in, the car you drive, the job you have. Who or what have you done it all for? Are you trying to please others, prove your worth, get somewhere and become someone? Or is there a sense of rebellion against your upbringing, and everything you do is the opposite of what those who held authority over you would have done?

There is a thread which runs through each individual and this is the intent by which we do everything. Intent can hide itself well, so question everything: why you say the things you say, walk in a particular way, how you eat your food and express yourself, etc. Because if you can look at the underlying reason as to why you do what you do, you will find a very important point within yourself and you will see how everything in you moves from this point.

The conscious is what you know about yourself, i.e. the descriptions of your personality, but the unconscious is just outside the grasp of conscious awareness. It is like an autonomous layer, which quietly works away, affecting your life. The content of the unconscious can often show itself through the dream state, but it is also the underlying reasons of why your life is as it is. The unconscious is your conditioning and hidden intent rising up into the conscious. If you were to observe yourself, all that is hidden in the unconscious would come out into the light and be consciously known.

If you were aware of all your intentions, you would no longer have an unconscious, because you would become very clear about why you do everything and what the pay-off is. You have lived the game of intent for most of your life and the realisation of how it works will lead you to taking a different action. Not an opposite action, as this means you are trying to run away from the conditioning, but rather an action that is beyond the realm of conditioning. For example, you realise how you habitually gossip about other people, simply because your unconscious intent is to make yourself feel better. Maybe you do this to cover over your feelings of inadequacy or because your life has been a struggle or empty?

Whatever the reason, once you see the intent behind your words, the next time you begin to gossip you realise why you are doing it. You do not berate yourself and say how bad you are for doing it and then go to the opposite of making the other person nice, which is trying to put 'right' the so-called 'wrong' you have done. Instead, you stop, and a silence occurs within you as you observe yourself. In this moment of stillness you know exactly the workings of your intent and you know what to do. This is action beyond the conditioning, beyond the mind.

The unconscious can only remain hidden if you let it. Once you start to observe your intent, all those hidden aspects will become known. This is self-knowledge and only you can do it. No spiritual leader, no society, counsellor, psychiatrist, doctor, healer or guru can do it for you. The only gift another person can give to you is to really listen, because this is an act of love. The rest is up to you and you have two choices: you either do it or you don't. If you don't, then you will carry on in the same vein of pain and suffering, if you do, then you will find out about you. *Once you know yourself, then you know every other human.*

Seducers and Parasites

Inside the game of intent you will find its driving force of seduction and parasitic wiles. Everything external in this world uses intent for luring in the commodity that will fulfil its desire. Intent exists externally 'out there' because it is an internal function within each individual. Take a look at all the people relevant in your life and ask yourself if you seduce them into getting what you want? In other words, what do you say and do in order to get someone to give you something? This something that you want could be energy, sympathy, joy, affection, praise, material possessions or even just a simple favour. Behind this act of seduction lies the intent. You are using someone else's fear or desire to get what you want.

Now look at all the times you have been seduced into giving something to someone. What is this person using in you in order to obtain what they want from you? Is it your fears, your desires, your generosity or even your naivety? How do you let them in? One of the most hidden factors people use is guilt, so how many times have you been seduced, or seduced others, through using subtle guilt? This is a crucial question because everyone is using seduction, consciously or unconsciously, to fulfil their desires.

Now look at the parasitic side of things. How many people do you feed off, or rely on? This could be through energy, support, money, attention, etc. Do you use seduction in order to be a parasite to draw on someone else's energy? Are you nice to someone to get something, yet the moment they turn their back all of your stored up frustration and anger surfaces? What is really going on? Feeding off another prevents you from being self-reliant, and allowing others to feed off you is also detrimental to your health. Look around you at all those people in your life who are parasitically drawing on your energy. In what ways do people feed off you and why do you let them?

Does this create a balanced and healthy relationship? If not, how can you stop playing the game of parasite and seduction, because once you see it and realise it, then you have just found the fodder that intent lives off. Therefore a huge chunk of your unconscious has just come out into the open to be healed.

Seductive and parasitic behaviours are being used by every institution and it even binds society and education together. Both of these institutions seduce and feed off individuals. Education prepares a child for society and society seduces it in order to feed itself. When you look at this whole process of just being a product to be used or using others, it is a shock, because everyone has intent and very few people are really sincere and open. Where you find any hierarchy, you will find this game at play. Even the well respected spiritual or business guru who demands your obedience to the dogmas of his beliefs is being seductive and you will bow down to him because you want to feed off his knowledge. This game can be blatant or it can be very subtle. The saddest thing of all is that humanity blindly accepts it and we allow it to continue through every vein of society and religion.

The human conditioning is a machine which trains you from birth to become something other than what you really are. It is a process of filling you up with the requirements of the machine in order to act according to its desires. You have become a slave and there is a strong pull in everyone to find out if there is a life that exists outside of the machine. We are having a relationship with each other and the world through hidden intent which is born from seductive and parasitic behaviour. Every generation was taught it and every generation passes it along. There are very few people who have stopped to ask what is really going on, who want to know what makes this world tick and why we do what we do. These are the people who have looked within themselves and seen their own part in the game and they have refused to play it.

When you take the blinkers from your eyes you see everything. It might not be a pleasant sight, but it is the truth and you deserve no less than the absolute truth, because then you are no longer a slave.

Self-Prostitution

We need money for the basic fundamentals in order to survive, so we trade our learnt knowledge for this commodity. This could be a fair trade, but in fact the whole monetary system has become polluted by corruption and greed and we often compromise ourselves in order to get money to survive in this vast machine of man-made society.

What exactly is prostitution? The word breaks down to describe something which is for sale. The most widely accepted social term for prostitution is that of selling the body for sex, but the real understanding of prostitution is an individual matter because on some level we are all doing it. Ask yourself exactly what you are selling to the world? It could be the sale of your gifts, your knowledge and your personal energy. Is the exchange fair, or are you giving yourself over to be used and abused by those who will take without care for any damage or responsibility?

Are you selling out of fear, desperation or need? We are all born with gifts and vital life-giving energy, but what would happen if you stopped selling that vital energy? Every thought, every act and every feeling is energy in movement. When you sell yourself for something in return you need to ask what will happen to the energy which you have sold. For example, if you are a weapon scientist and you are selling your knowledge to make equipment that can kill millions of so-called enemies and destroy nature, then you have to be very clear on how your energy has gone into that product and moved outwards, making you a part of every murdering bullet or bomb. This is the responsibility of selling yourself. This applies to everyone no matter how inconsequential you believe your energy to be. This energy exchange happens whether we are consciously aware of it or not. We are not just living a human materialistic life, we are spiritual beings. You may argue this fact, but just because you cannot see air does not prove its non-existence.

When we look outside of our windows we can honestly say nature has, without a doubt, been prostituted by humanity.

Heartbreakingly, we never asked her permission for anything, we just took, nor have we traded fairly and this is called rape. Almost everything we have done and taken from her has resulted in a cry of protest. We are not separate from nature, but we believe we are. We kill animals, pollute the oceans, rivers and the air, we drill great big holes in her and we fill her with filthy rubbish. We have even claimed her land and put up fences and called a scrappy piece of acreage 'mine' and then we have the cheek to sell it to other humans for huge amounts of money, just so they too can call it their own, yet in truth we have never owned it. It is an illusion.

What right have we got to abuse something so life-giving? When will we realise we are being abusive to the one thing which has given us the ability to live on this planet? She has given each of us a human body and the bounty of nature was laid at our feet. We came here to help her and work with her, yet she has suffered at the hands of humanity. If you were to really look at nature you would see that there is something so deeply wrong. If a God supposedly created this Earth and nature, then why are there acts of non-love here? An animal killing another animal, a plant strangling another plant, birds pinching eggs from other nests, etc. If God is all-loving, how could he possibly create a non-loving energy? How can love create non-love? Is that possible, or has something else happened which we are ignorant of?

We came here as humans to sort out the problem, not make it worse. We have become so caught up in the games of society, religion, money and position that we have stopped doing what we were supposed to do. Nature is the proof of that. She is in a terrible state and slowly dying at our hands, simply because we prostituted her and now we have become her fat rich pimp.

Whatever we do externally, we are doing internally, so the abuse of nature in the world is the abuse of our own inner self. How many times have we traded the very beauty of our essence of pure light to get something materialistic or to have security? Is this an act of love or an act of fear? Is the actual fear of not being able to survive here and the fear of death driving us to sell our spiritual heritage to the darker basal desires of the human mind?

We are conditioned from birth, right through to the day we die. We live life from rules set down by institutions, which add and subtract limitations through each generation. We follow blindly, whilst we suffer at the same time. Will this conditioning ever stop? Because it is not the solution to the healing of humanity and this planet, as each generation is getting more restless and more destructive, and we can see this happening in music, films, technology, media, food, alcohol and material possessions. Humanity is insatiable and it keeps on desiring more and more. Underneath this greed is fear. It is the fear of not knowing which keeps us driving forward for a security that does not exist.

The root of the human conditioning is this very same fear. It is deeply embedded in the soil of duality, which is right and wrong, pleasure and pain. Each child is brought up according to this model which is outlined by its nation. We are teaching our children separation from each other and we are teaching them to live from the mind, fear and learnt descriptions. This is because we are doing it to ourselves. Somewhere along the way we abandoned our connection to the real 'us' and now we are lost. Well, there is a way out of the mire of illusion; you just have to be prepared to drop your conditioning. Not through years of therapy, but through seeing the very fact of this conditioning, and the very fact is, you have become something other than what you really are.

Chapter 4

Is Religion Whole or is it Divided?

If you look at this world it is divided on so many levels and one of those divisions is religion. Each religion has its own path of guiding people to its so-called truth and the only reason why people seek religion is that they cannot find the truth inside themselves, or they have been conditioned from birth to accept a religion. The external has become the solution and they look to someone in supposed authority to tell them how to find God or what is going to happen after death. People have become more concerned about what position or rewards they will get when they die than what happens when they are alive. Sadly, they no longer pay attention to life.

What Exactly is Religion?

How many religions are there? Or how many various beliefs and philosophies do we have to choose from in order to find God? There is Catholicism, Christianity, Islam, Sufism, Buddhism, Judaism, Hinduism, and there are many more. Out of these religions the New Age has emerged with its angels, gurus, reiki, crystals, paganism, rituals, star-gods, etc. Each religion and new age concept has a path to enlightenment and a hierarchical system of authority.

The second you choose to become part of a belief or a system, you have immediately become separated from all those outside of this belief. Religion does not unite the world, it separates it, and anything that separates is not an act of love. Ask yourself if this is true. If religion united people, then why is there a terrorist war, or why is Islam at war with the Jews and the Hindus? If each religion is the so-called way to God in order to become enlightened, then why do so few people get make it? Would an enlightened person kill another human being? Or is it just a system of elitism?

Religion is not working, because if it were we would all be God-realised beings on this planet, working in harmony with each other and with nature. In fact, we are nowhere near to reaching this concept. Historically, religion has helped us to separate and divide families, towns, cities, countries, nations and ultimately the world. People die and kill over their beliefs. The whole concept of heaven and hell has held the majority of people in a deadly trap. If there is such a thing as God, would he really be proud of what we do in the name of religion? Would he advocate this separation saying it is necessary in order to find him? If so, is this an act of love? Would love kill, maim, abuse, discipline, control and dominate? If you answer no to this question, then why do we continue to give religion the power that it has on this Earth? Only a mind would do these things.

In the beginning, who or what created religions? Nearly all the major religions were created after the death of their inspired originator. The only major religion to be created by the person himself was Islam. Mohammed's revelations of Allah, the One God, were collected shortly after his death into a volume called the Koran. His statements became a set of rules for a supposed peaceful way of living. All the books that underpin any religion have been written in language and where does language come from? It is a learnt description from the mind and we have held fast onto this written descriptive word, giving it authority over our lives and we even kill for it. We have become subservient to human thought. We have given over our personal power to a belief created by a human mind whose only desire is to control through a very cleverly organised system of hierarchy and power.

Christianity was formed after the death of Jesus, creating a religion filled with worship and dogma, but his life message was reported to be based on his simple teachings of 'the kingdom of heaven is within you', and 'love your brother as yourself'. Buddha reportedly said at the end of his life, 'seek your own salvation', but very few listened, as a system was built around the life of this one man, affecting millions of people. So who or what is really creating this whole movement of religion? Why would the human being need so many rules, rituals and dogmas? Surely you can feel within yourself if it would be uncomfortable to murder, steal and lie. Are we so far removed from our own inner sense of truth that we need an external power to tell us, and in exchange they get to control and dominate us? Isn't this self-prostitution, seduction and parasitic behaviour?

Religion is responsible for millions of deaths worldwide over thousands of years. Documented history describes the brutal murders of those people who refused to convert to various religious orders, yet people still have faith in the power of such institutions. Only a human mind could create something so vile. Would love kill millions of people because they refused to love? Would that be an act of love? Murder is not an act of love. How can religion portray itself to be based on a foundation of love if it is the cause of so much world violence, or is it in fact built on manipulation and hierarchy? It is one of the richest businesses on this planet and it manufactures the illusion that people need an intermediary to reach God. The abbots, gurus, priests, vicars, bishops and archbishops are all in the 'know' as to the workings of God. The general people need to be 'taught' as they do not have direct communication.

You may argue about all of this and say how religion is necessary, because underneath all the hierarchy, division, war and corruption you believe it has good foundations. You may say it is man himself who has corrupted religion and that originally it was based on pure intent. We have come back to the same point of intent. How can intent be pure if its driving force is seduction and parasitic behaviour? Knowing this, what was the real reason behind creating religion? This is what we want answered, because millions are separated from each other because of belief systems and they are trapped by the dogmas and the rules of worship.

To most people God is outside of themselves and he is something which needs to be found by searching and taking a spiritual path. They often feel they are not worthy enough to know him or they are waiting for a second saviour to come and lead the way. Why? How come a person can often look at a flower unfolding and see the majesty of life, yet they cannot see the same essence within themself? What has got in the way?

What Keeps Us Tied to Religion?

Religion is an institution which educates people on the subject of spiritual matters. It tries to define why we are human, the purpose for living and the journey 'back' to God. It was created by the mind and the mind can only live and work in opposites, so in every religion you will find there is God and then there is its opposite. Some call this the devil, satan, etc., and others describe it as the traps of basal human desire and so forth. Most people are afraid they will end up being captured by this opposing force, so they 'try' to be 'good' in order to get into the heavenly spheres of God.

Each religion has a definition of what being 'good' for their God entails. Some have a wrathful vengeful God and others have a merciful God, etc. Some religions describe a nameless God who can only be reached by attaining a state where thought has ceased, so they 'train' their minds to become still, silent and meditative, but what exactly is 'training' the mind to become quiet? Is it the mind itself? If so, then have they really moved out of the mind?

There may also be some very beautiful aspects to religion. For some people it draws out their creativity or gives them something secure to anchor to and they use it as a means of comfort. Many people turn to religion when they have been close to death or when a loved one dies. They start the search for proof of life after death. This thread of belief that we go on living after the body dies runs through most religions. The Buddhists prepare for their next life by the good deeds of this life. The Christians and Catholics do good works to get into heaven and avoid hell. Some Muslims fight for their cause and die in the process to be exalted in heaven with thirty virgins, etc., but these 'beliefs' are not divine; they are just plain and simple human, yet we have fought and killed over them.

Each religion works on divide and rule, as each one claims to have the right way to God and salvation. No wonder we have mass confusion. If religions are at war with other religions, what does this say about the love and peace that they advocate? It says: underneath all their doctrines, their disciplines and their rules, there is antagonism and hatred. Do we really want this in our lives? Are they showing us the brotherhood of man or are we just pawns in a huge political game? The human family is a fragmented family. All we can do is see this as a fact.

Even the atheists have a problem because they believe that God does not exist. This means they are at the opposite end of duality, so to denounce and rebel is not the solution either. This belief or non-belief of God is just a mental concept, which is shaped by all your life experiences and the power others have over you. What if you dropped all the beliefs and just observed life and nature? Surely the truth would reveal itself? We cannot do this though, because a belief in something gives us a blanket of security.

What is Religion Really Selling to Us?

What is this security which we get from religion? Do our beliefs in God, a second coming of Christ or Maitreya bring us only a direction and a focus for the mind, or is it just another way to escape this vast sense of loneliness? What would it mean for you if all your fears and psychological babble ended? Would it mean a boring life without any drama? If so, are you confirming how the mind would be bored by being just a tool to be used in terms of practical reference? It is the mind which craves experiences and the dramas they bring. Many philosophies describe these dramas as acts of karma and they state how karma is the very thing which keeps us returning to this planet by the route of reincarnation. If this is true, does this mean we are caught up in the endless rounds of living life as a human being until we can get to the point where our every act is an act of love? Therefore, the mind would have to be dealt with in the end, because it has created your past and it will build your future on the wheel of pleasure and pain, which is not love.

Ultimately, the real fear is all about death and the unknown. Are you afraid of your own death or the death of your family? Would you like to know that you and they go to another place where you can all be safe and be together again? This yearning to know if we exist beyond death is something the mind strives for. Death is the unknown and the mind is all the gathered information of the known. We cannot see beyond the veil of death and this frustrates the mind.

To find answers to this huge question, we seek out various mediums, psychics and clairvoyants for proof of life after death, or we immerse ourselves in religion or philosophies where we may be guaranteed a good place after death according to our devotion to God and the beneficial works we have done on the Earth. For those who believe in reincarnation this also guarantees them a better 'next life', but those unfortunate people who have done evil deeds can only look forward to an eternal life after death in hell and flames. Even the atheists will have a problem, because although they can be guaranteed the job of becoming worm food and generating the good soil of the Earth and disperse into nothingness, which is just another belief system, they are also responsible for mass murder, conquering and converting others on this planet, so how will they face the consequences of their actions if there is no afterlife for them?

What we need to be clear about in all of this is the truth. Throughout your life you have been given and also claimed many labels about yourself. This is who you have become and it has nothing to do with who you actually are. All these labels are a mind-made description, which forms an image of you. This image holds all your thoughts, past experiences, likes, dislikes, opinions, fears and emotions, and people know it as the personality. Therefore, when you die, what will happen to these descriptions or your personality? Surely they will go back to its creator, which is the mind.

This means every thought you have had is held within Total Mind and this Mind holds every other single human thought. It is a huge egregore which lives within and around the whole material Universe. This is how mediums and psychics tap into other life forms and the personalities of deceased people. They are tapping into the Mind and finding the imprint of the personality's life on the Earth. Once you know how this works you can speak to any personality within the Mind, dead or alive. When you were born you did not have any learnt behaviour, therefore there was no personality, yet you were still alive, so beyond mind there is something else that lives and when you die, it returns to its place which exists beyond the mind.

The mind wants to live after death. It wants all that collected history, all of its labels and beliefs to continue into another place, but in reality, it is not the real you. For example, your grandfather dies, but what has really died? His body, his personality, his beliefs, his conditioning and his labels have died and if it is this which you have loved, then effectively you have loved his mind, which created his personality. You have loved only his illusionary self and not the real thing behind it that was covered up by mind, society and religion.

Look around you and you will realise you have spent your whole life either liking or disliking people's personalities. The same principle applies to you. Therefore, have you ever really loved and been truly loved in return or have you just been having a relationship with illusion? There is no right or wrong in loving a personality, what I am asking is: can you see the truth of a person and yourself beyond what they and you have become? If you can realise the truth a shift will occur within you and you will see it in its totality. When you love another and yourself from this point onwards, you will do it without any illusion or attachment to the personality. This thing that lives on, which is not formed by the mind, is the same thing that exists in you and in another person. There is no separation, no me, no you, no we, no us, just the one thing.

Personalities are separate because they all have different past history which shapes the human being. Therefore, the mind creates separation between one person and the next. The life, which exists beyond the mind, is not separate. This is true love. Do you need the institutions of religion to find this out? Do you need a security blanket, a comfort zone? Only the mind needs this. You, the real you beyond personality, continues to live.

What Would Happen to Religion If...?

If the top Buddhist leaders, the leaders of Islam, New Age, Hinduism, Judaism and the hierarchy of all Christian faiths, including the atheists, realised the folly and dropped their beliefs, what would happen? Would the Buddhist become enlightened? Would the Christians realise that the truth will set them free from the institutions of hierarchy and power? Would all others free themselves of their rituals and start to love all humans and not just the selective few? If you put all these leaders in a room together, would they try to convert each other? If they were then led inside themselves to the point of truth and they dropped their illusions, how would this affect their relationship to each other? Would there be a necessity to convert anyone? Would religion continue to exist?

You can have communication with this life that lives within you right now. You do not have to go to anyone else, follow anyone else, believe anyone else or go anywhere else. It is right here, right now and it is personal to you. This life, which makes your heart beat, will share every moment with you and it knows you intimately. The cross on the church altar is a piece of dead wood or metal, it does not know you, nor does it care about you. No-one but this life knows you, because you are it and it is you. Mind has taken you on a journey as far away from it as it possibly can. Why? How come the mind has control of you and ultimately this world? What does it want? Who or what actually invented the mind and controls it? We need to know because something has got in the way of love.

Religion is not built on love because it has murdered and led people into separation and elitism. What would happen if religion ended today? Most wars would definitely cease and people would be faced with their ultimate fear of being alone and held within the void of the unknown. No-one knows if God truly exists or if there is a set path to finding him, because the second you say you know, you have entered into the mind. Self-discovery is endless and timeless and that is the beauty of it. Never be fooled by the masks that people wear, because they too have been conditioned.

What is the Great Mystery?

The Egyptians were a remarkable race and they built their initiation temples in order to be free from the traps of this Earth and Universe. One particular temple, Karnak in Luxor, actually mocks humanity. The moment you enter this temple you will stand amidst huge statues and columns, and as you walk further in you will find prayer rooms, smaller initiation temples and ritual chambers dedicated to various Gods. Thousands of years ago people were encouraged to pray here and leave their gifts to the Gods, but only the high priests and pharaohs were allowed into the hidden chambers, which included the Osirion.

Once you have walked the length and width of the temple and discovered all the nooks and crannies of the chambers, if you are lucky you will come to a small enclosure, which is often used by the Egyptian officials as a toilet. On the wall of this room you will find a carving which describes the actual purpose of life. It shows how all the initiations and rituals are pointless and the picture reveals the tree of life. It says that the way to freedom is through each individual.

All the huge statues, chambers and carvings were placed as egoic symbols; they appeased the mind. The actual truth of human life was in a toilet at the back. It took apart all the hierarchy, dogmas and initiations and left you standing simply as your true self. This is what was known by some pharaohs. If you were able to see through the illusion of the temple and you demanded to be shown, you were led to this room. Those who got stuck on the doctrines never saw the inside of the Osirion and so they stayed in the illusion of the many Gods.

The great mystery is that there is no mystery. It is all about you. Every person who has found the truth out for themselves have said the same thing, 'It is within you.' It is even written on the Greek temple at Delphi, 'Know yourself and then you will know the Universe and the Gods.' It is that simple.

Part One Summary

The acknowledgment

We wanted to see where we are as a human race and we know that if we continue in the same way, there will no longer be a human race left. We murder, we hate, we fear and we are conditioned. We also help each other, create beautiful things and we have courage, but all these things are held within the opposite traits which live within the mind.

The mind is king on this planet and it will take a great deal of individual energy to dismantle its power. Mind must become the servant and not the master and this is essential for the well-being of all existence. You, as the individual, need to stop and look at yourself as you are and acknowledge the illusion which has got you caught up on the wheel of the mind.

From what you have read so far can you acknowledge the following:

1. The world is in chaos.
2. You add to this chaos through your beliefs and your conditioning.
3. You are caught in the trap of society because you are striving to be something other than what you are.
4. Society is based on hierarchy, power and wealth.
5. Your mind works on the principles of pleasure and pain.
6. You seduce others and you have been seduced.
7. You play the game of parasitic behaviours.
8. You do these things because you have hidden intent and desires.
9. Religion separates and divides the human family.
10. You have formed images and judgments about yourself and others and these are what keep you separate.

Or are you defending, attacking and forming opinions about what you have read in this book? Have any of these crossed your mind:

1. The world is in chaos because other people are to blame.
2. I have not been conditioned and I try to live a good life, so no, I am not adding to the chaos.
3. Society is there to help us and protect us. If people are suffering then it is their own fault and nothing to do with me.
4. If you earn prestige and position, what is wrong with that?
5. I cannot see how a person can live without a mind even if it is created by duality. I am my thoughts and my mind.
6. I have my reasons as to why I do what I do to get what I want.
7. I am not parasitic on anyone. Everyone relies on me to help them.
8. Desire and intent is normal. Everyone has them. Does that make me bad to want nice things?
9. I believe in God and religion is my spiritual right. I go to church to worship with other like-minded people, who also believe in God. Yes, religion creates wars, but I don't play a part in that bit of religion, so therefore it has nothing to do with me.
10. I can't live without image. I am one person when I'm with my parents and another person when I'm with my friends because that's what we expect from each other. I can't be the son in front of my friends, it wouldn't be right.

Before we can move on to Part Two, you have to have seen the illusion which keeps every human separate from each other. The mind, society and religion are responsible for the state of this world, but it first began in each individual. The solution must therefore begin with each individual and that individual is you.

You may at this point feel despair or removed from any notion of hope. There may be a sense of standing alone without any support around you because society and religion can no longer be depended on for the truth. You may have become disheartened as you realise you are conditioned, opinionated and judgmental and now you do not feel as though you can trust what your mind is telling you. You have been living in illusion for so long and when you see it as a fact it will create a shock. Everything you have held as a belief is being taken apart because it was created by a mind which lives on pleasure and pain. There is no love in belief, as love does not have pleasure or pain within it, and so it lives beyond the illusion.

If you cannot acknowledge the illusion at this point, then I advise you not to continue upon the journey in this book, as it is not the truth you seek, but a mind-based path. The inner cry of passion for the ending of all human suffering needs to be felt in order to continue into Part Two. If you have not felt this and you read on, seeking only knowledge, then you will find yourself challenged even more, because the next step takes you into a world as minute as the cell within your body and as vast as the cosmos.

Part Two

Who Am I?

Chapter 5

Separating the Truth from the Illusion

When you can accept yourself for who you are without trying to be a 'somebody' in the eyes of humanity, then you have let go of your ego. Only an ego would make a person a 'somebody' or its opposite, a 'nobody'. Your descriptive labels are not who you are, they are what you have become, so don't judge yourself and others on the value of a label. Instead, allow the true you to emerge, because when you are not attached to any descriptive label, you are free.

Let's Start at the Very Beginning.

Before you can look at the root cause of a situation you have to first stop and admit to yourself that there is a problem. If you live in denial over an issue or get frustrated by blaming those around you for your predicament, then the problem will never get resolved. All of your conditioning has confused you as to the 'whole' way to live. You are divided internally, which reflects externally, when dealing with daily situations and problems.

In reality, the mind has actually taken over, and it is acting sporadically between two poles – opposites – and you are constantly making decisions based on your opinions of 'good' or 'bad' and not on fact. The mind is working separately from intuition or the inner voice, which would lead you through the illusion and into the truth. The inner voice encompasses all, so it does not move as a separate entity to the inner voice within another person, as it has no central place from where it moves, but mind moves according to individual conditioning, which includes your beliefs, opinions, judgments, culture, nationality, education, etc., and this separating movement creates a central 'I' or egoic mind. This central point, where the egoic mind has its root, is based on desire and fear, and it wants to keep itself safe and so it seeks only pleasure whilst trying to avoid any pain. This self-seeking is what causes the separation between one human and another, which is an act of non-love.

If the majority of humans are living from their individual egoic mind, then desire and fear-based thought must collect together as an energy and link up with their originator, namely, 'total mind', so within the ether and space, there must be this collected egregore of all thought, (thought, which, on this planet, creates society and religion). Individual mind is the egoic mind, and total mind is the collection of all human, nature and all thoughts from other life-forms added together.

To understand the workings of your individual egoic mind in order to live beyond it, you will need to break it down and see all of its elements. This will show you how it is functioning in your life, and how the egoic mind was created. Every human

70

has an egoic mind, which is unique to them due to the person's life circumstances, but if you can find it in you and see it in action for yourself, you will gain self-knowledge and with this comes the realisation of how you can bring deep fundamental change to your life and the world, yet all you did was look within yourself.

Even after being presented with the many forms of self-development, which deals with this issue or that issue, there are still billions of people who are crying out for help to find a way through the mire of suffering which living on this planet brings. Even if a person meets a self-aware person, who informs them that the only solution is to look within at the way they are thinking and acting, they often shun this significant undertaking and continue to weep for an external answer. Humanity has been advised countless times to 'look within', but very few take the challenge. People want something solid and material or a handbook of instructions. They want a quick fix, so that they can apply the so-called 'solution' and then continue in the same vein of pursuing pleasure and rejecting pain.

Over recent decades the urgency to become more aware and responsible for our environment and live a balanced life has become plainly obvious. We have been adding to the pollution of the planet for thousands of years and it is growing each year. When this fact has been presented to the majority, some have raised their hands in response and said, 'Well, what can I do about it?' This 'victim syndrome' of feeling powerless to change the world is what keeps us caught on the merry-go-round of worthlessness. You are the creator of your own life. You have drawn towards you all of your experiences because of the deep-rooted fear which resides within your being. *You* and only *you* can change your life, not by thinking differently or by focusing on positive thinking, but by going within and eradicating fear. There is no other way and any external solution is only a temporary fix.

The antidote to the poison of the egoic mind is to face it and see it for what it is, but many people get angry and they want to belittle the inner journey to peace. This rejection of the

71

inner life often creates a sense of hopelessness and people can become suspicious of each other, always waiting for the other person to cause them pain, or they become the abuser by using others to get ahead at any cost. This using others, or the feelings of being used, creates a wall of isolation, and many begin to hold life at arms length in order to feel self-protected.

Some people try to counter-act this sense of separation by becoming overly demanding or possessive, trying to get love from others, because the feeling of being hollow is all too engulfing. The opposite of this controlling behaviour is to be excessively accommodating with the aim of pleasing others at the expense of the giver's inner peace. This temporarily satisfies the desire to be accepted as a worthy human being, but sooner or later the feelings of being 'not good enough' will resurface.

When you stop and admit what you are doing to yourself and others, you will feel a great chasm of loneliness. You can no longer look to any external authority to guide you through this uncharted land, as most humans are too caught up in the conditioning of the mind, society and religion, so they do not know how to help you. Society would tell you to strive and become a 'somebody'. The mind would give you a solution in terms of good or bad, and religion would answer you with its illusionary gods and fake security. None of these is going to help you because these are the traps of humanity. You are going to have to help yourself, and to do that you will need to become what you most fear: vulnerable.

Your daily life is probably made up from a sequence of routines, which may include responsibility, work, family, financial ups and downs, expectations, desires and numerous emotions. These routines you create will generally revolve around security and the avoidance of the unknown. The unknown is situated outside of your safe habitual living and you instinctively feel that if you enter into the unknown it will bring you face-to-face with what you fear. For example, going somewhere unfamiliar, sitting next to a stranger on the bus, ignoring an intuitive impulse because it means taking a risk, remaining silent at work even though you need help, speaking up for yourself, saying no, and so on. Instead of getting real and facing all what is not at peace, you just trudge along in relative safety until eventually you will meet the great unknown, which is death, but that is some time in the future, so you do not need to look at that right now, do you?

This safe and orderly manufactured 'you' is generally living only ten per cent of its potential, because a huge chunk of its power is missing. This power is not something that can be found in any external success or pleasure, it can only be found from within, but we are too afraid to harness this power and so we run away from it. To be in this power means we have to live life from a point of fearlessness, which involves living from a point of absolute truth, and this will have an effect on our current life conditions. To live beyond the traps of humanity and its pain and suffering, you have to know yourself intimately. Every movement, from your thoughts, to your suppressed fears, intents and desires have to be observed and the actual root of them has to be faced. It is therefore important to start at, and understand, the very beginning of life itself.

The Atom

The physicist, Georges Lemaître, in explaining the origins of material creation, proposed 'the hypothesis of the primeval atom', more commonly known as the 'Big Bang Theory'. He declared that all life came from the one atom and described the universe coming to life as 'the cosmic egg exploding at the point of creation'.

If you esoterically look inside the primeval atom, you will find a magnetic field of three key things: negatively charged electrons, which we know as the female pulling force, positively charged protons, known as the male pushing force, and non-electrically charged neutrons, which are referred to as the inner voice. The neutron itself is the heart and intelligence of the atom and it has no opposing magnetic pull or push.

The atomic bomb is created by removing the electron or the female from the atom, producing an all male environment, which creates an expansion or explosion. Therefore, at the very point of the initial eruption, the female was not actually within the energy which burst forth. The atom, as we know it, was essentially created as the male rushed outwards and hit the still and silent female energy of the unmanifest. This union caused the exploding male to be pulled into her vast space, creating the primeval atom. The second the heat of the active male touched the cold of the passive female a magnitude of chemicals and molecules formed and material life was born, bringing a new Universe into existence. Some of the chemicals that were born of this union were non-toxic, but when fused with other chemicals they became toxic substances and so a distortion also began to ripple through material existence.

Esoterically, the explanation for the creation of life has been known for thousands of years. There are references to it in the bible, but there were many past philosophers and teachers who understood how 'God' was unmanifest intelligence, resting in his infinite silence, which is often referred to as the 'womb or female'. From out of Himself he poured into the womb his male seed or a likeness of Himself in the form of his 'Son' and together his Son and the womb created life.

The primeval atom is therefore male, female, and also has the intelligence of the original creator in the form of the neutral, so every cell within your body has this primeval atom, which consists of these three components. Even if you are a female or male in the external human form, you will still have both of them residing within the cells. The organs also reflect this as they work like a magnet, pulling and pushing, so the macrocosm of the universe is actually the microcosm in you.

Physicists have recently stated that before the original atom was created, all of its electrons, protons and neutrons were not divided, they were one particle, and when they were observed using particle colliders, they faded into a non-material state. We will cover this in more depth in part three, but it does bring forward a very important question: are there two ways to exist? Is there a permanent immaterial existence and an impermanent material existence? Science is proving that both do exist, so are we living two lives at the same time? If we have access to the immaterial intelligence through the neutral in the cell, and the point is to live life from who we really are, then what was the point in creating material impermanence in the first place?

Who or What Created the Atom?

If what created the atom was material and physical, then it would have a beginning and an end to its life and it would have within it the energy of separation. Gravity, time and the mind were created at the point of the male explosion, as there was now a space or room for movement between the active male and the passive female, creating magnetic points of opposite poles. This means that if the original creator was a material being, then there would be a space where a material and mental path would reside in order to reach it. The mind would therefore be aware of it and everyone would have a clear direction on how to attain it.

Humanity is currently confused because the mind does not know where the creator really is, so it has created many paths to it with a supposed end result of attaining some sort of God-like consciousness. In truth the creator is not a material or physical 'thing', so it cannot be grasped by thinking, nor is there a tangible place to go and meet it. This means the source of the original atom must be non-materialistic and permanent, as its creator is not something which can be reached within the material spheres of physicality. This elusive thing which everyone is searching for cannot be found through the material, impermanent mind.

This now releases the human from all the meaningless mental and physical searching we do, as any form of image worship, seeking nirvana, or concentration and meditation are all illusions, because the mind, which is a material entity, cannot enter into the immaterial. You cannot step into the unknown with the mind, because the mind functions in opposites and memory, which is the known. Thought cannot function in a space where there is no separating entity. In order to cross the threshold the mind must become that which it is trying to enter into, or it will be annihilated.

The key to freedom is therefore within the mind itself and the understanding of what exactly it is doing in each and every moment. If we can understand the mind and see it in its totality, then we can end the constant battle with the opposites of pleasure and pain. This cessation is what will allow us to actually penetrate into the world of the unknown and see the self for what it really is.

The movement of 'becoming', or evolution, exists within the material spheres, and over eons of time it has found a place to reside in the human psychological desire to strive and achieve. It is this very movement which creates the division and fragmentation between the male and the female within the atom, and also externally in relationships. The constant battle within, between good and bad or pleasure and pain, are what prevent these two principles from moving as one.

The Cortex

The largest organ in the human body which shows the workings of the atom is the brain. There is the female right hemisphere, which governs the left side of the body and intuitive responses, and the male left hemisphere, which governs the right side of the body and logical programming, and the cortex, which is the neutral and observation between feeling and logic. Surrounding the cortex are nerves and tissue which hold memory and if a person damages these, then a loss of memory occurs.

These nerves not only store knowledge on how to function chronologically on this planet, but they also store all of our past scenarios, our fears and our desires for the future. Each time you encounter a physical experience or recall something from memory, information passes over the cortex in the form of thoughts. The cortex responds to the passing information by jumping up to meet it and depositing your life-giving energy into it. The thought, which is now full of vitality, spends this energy by expanding itself, and after it passes over the cortex it continues on a journey by either creating future scenarios or re-playing past events. This is the constant flow of mental chatter and if a person lives mostly in their thinking then they will have a very busy mind.

If you are to understand yourself then it is important to deal with the hindering activity of your thoughts which are taking this vital energy. The cortex can therefore help you, as the actual awareness of this process taking place can cause you to empty your memory banks, releasing you from living a life dictated by your thoughts. For example, I am describing to you an experience I recently had on an aeroplane. The information goes through your ears and hits your memory banks which surround your cortex, and because like attracts like, you start to remember your aeroplane incidents. Even whilst I am still talking you are playing your aeroplane memories around in your head and you are working out what you are going to say when I have finished. You are no longer listening – you are thinking, and the moment I end my chatter, you jump straight in with your story.

The key is to catch the moment when a memory has been triggered by the conversation. At this point you can allow the thoughts to rise, but instead of getting caught up in the flow of your memories and working out what to say next, you just let the thoughts move through you. By not giving the thoughts any attention or energy, you will notice how they fade away.

This split-second realisation and observation of your mind will naturally cause you to go back to listening. You are actually emptying your memory banks without effort and therefore you are not wasting your vital energy. The cortex remains at peace, as it no longer reaches up to grab the memory and it has become like a lake and your thoughts are the geese flying overhead, but even though the geese cast their reflection upon the water, they do not disturb the surface. When you get caught up in thought, the surface becomes turbulent.

This does not mean that you cannot share with another person. You can still tell your aeroplane story should you choose to do so, but it will be from a point of observation and listening and not from the assessing, analyzing and judging mind. The truth is, you cannot think and listen at the same time. You can think and hear, but you cannot think and listen. Listening is when you are totally attentive to the person with your whole being, and this attentiveness creates stillness without any effort. For example, when you watch a beautiful sunset, listen to a piece of music or look into the face of a newborn, you step into a space where past and future no longer dominate the moment. Therefore, listening is an act of love, so if you want to love someone, totally listen to them.

The second you catch yourself following the train of your thoughts, bring yourself back to the awareness of it. If you find you are labelling yourself as bad for getting caught up in the stream of your thoughts, then this is a self-judgment and your thoughts will respond by bringing up all the times in the past when you were bad, and off you go again. Observing yourself without judgment will reveal what your mind does and how it is always trying to attract your attention and take you off someplace else, away from the moment. A still mind is a quiet mind and it no longer gets distracted by the constant chattering of human thought.

This vital energy thought uses is meant to be in the body in order for you to fully function on the Earth. It is your spiritual heritage, but if it is being used by the mind, then your whole being will be affected and eventually you will end up drained, ill or burnt out. Thought has its own place as a tool for assimilating information. The spiritual energy you have is meant to be fully immersed in every cell within your body and radiate out into nature. If it never gets past the brain then you are not radiating it, you are in fact weak in the spiritual sense, as you will live only from the experiences of the mind. This lack of energy will drive you to take energy from those around you and you will do this by using the game of intent, i.e. manipulation and seduction, etc. This may be done consciously or unconsciously, but either way you will be working towards taking the life-giving force from another. This will feed and sustain your addiction to thought, but it is parasitic behaviour in action.

Awareness of the cortex is therefore a crucial key in getting to know yourself intimately, and by observing your thoughts you have taken a huge step to self-liberation. The shift of power from being an autonomous thinking being, to a being who observes the autonomous egoic mind, is spiritual intelligence in action. You are no longer in the thought, you are watching the thought and something very subtle is happening. You have in fact stepped out of the trap and you are now watching it from the sidelines.

Male, Female, Neutral: the Atom within the Body Cell

There has been so much written on the topic of the ego or egoic mind, but very few people know what it is, how it was created and where it resides within the body. From the point of birth we are programmed by the people around us and the environment, and we store this programmed information in the nerves that surround the cortex, and in the individual cells which make up the blood and organs of the body. The main prominent role models for most people are the mother and father.

If you were to write a list of all the negative and positive beliefs which your mother has about life, and then those of your father, and finally your own, you will find you have taken some beliefs from each and made them your point of reality. If you continue to hold these patterns and live by them, then your life will eventually reflect theirs and you will live in a similar vein. If you write a list of the beliefs which you are giving to your children, you will also see how you are passing on various conditioned beliefs down the generations. These will shape their lives and they will pass them on and so forth.

The most dynamic relationship, which reveals a lot about our self, is the relationship we have with our partner. If you were to write a list of your partner's or your recent ex-partner's positive and negative beliefs, you will realise that in actual fact you are describing yourself. Your closest external relationship is a reflection of what is stored in your atoms and ultimately in your cells. For example, if my partner is a strong male, or if I am in a same-sex relationship where he/she is playing the more dominant role, then what I believe about my partner is stored in the male aspect of my atoms. If I am a submissive female and I have a list of the things I believe are good and bad about myself, then I have stored these in the female component of my atoms.

Whatever sex you are, what you believe about your gender self goes into the same sex in the atom, and the beliefs about your partner go in the opposite sex in the atom. Even if you are a strong female, reflecting the more authoritarian qualities of a male, you will draw to you a partner who reflects the more female aspect of you, because ultimately there is an imbalance between the atomic inner male and female which reside within the cells.

Most negative beliefs about the female revolve around the issues of being weak and vulnerable, and the positive traits often include the ability to nurture and express creatively. The negative opinions about the male usually centre upon a lack of trust, and anger issues and the positive qualities often reflect his ability to protect, and take action.

These positive and negative beliefs about yourself and what you believe about your partner are actually revealing your egoic mind. It is all the stored conditioning: pleasure, pain, opinions and judgments, which you have collected as memory within your atoms, thus affecting your cells, and there is a battle between the male and female about which one gets to express itself at any given time. Each moment brings forth another experience which you get to store as either good or bad according to your learnt beliefs, so you are constantly adding and subtracting beliefs.

The conditioned you or central 'I', which is the egoic mind, has been taught to behave according to what is acceptable socially and to reject all that is not termed as 'good'. You have within you a male and a female and you will know if you are at war internally, because your external relationship will have some sort of communication problem. Your partner is you, and any problems that lie between you are issues which need to be first sorted out within yourself. Once you take action on these non-loving aspects of yourself, then the outer relationship will also go through a change.

Diagram 1: The positive and negative beliefs stored in the primeval atom.

The outer shell of the atom.

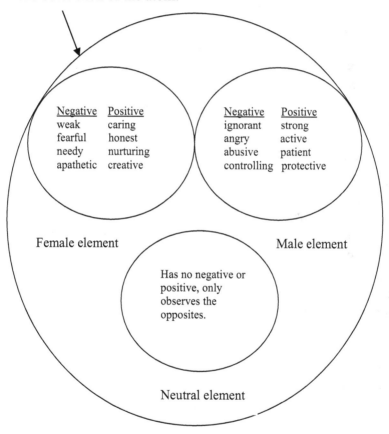

One human cell holds more than one hundred trillion atoms, which form together to create various elements, i.e. oxygen, hydrogen, magnesium, etc. This means every chemical element in the body is being affected by electrons, protons and neutrons which eventually create and sustain all the organs within the body. Therefore, your conditioning, which is stored trillions of times over in one cell, is affecting all the living organisms which make up your human life. Diagram 1 focuses on the original primeval atom, which according to what you program into it, evolves into the sum total of your personality and the state of your physical body. Release the conditioning and you will affect an unimaginable number of atoms, which in turn affects the totality of 'you' and therefore the world.

If you look at the neutral element in the diagram, you will see how it does not store any positive and negative opinions. It is the constant observer, which watches the battle between the two opposites. The neutral is intelligence, because it is not swayed by negative or positive, therefore it does not work in opposites. If there is no movement within it, then it must have the element of silence or space. Its true function is to find the fact of a situation and move within that fact. You know when you are operating outside of the truth when you describe an outcome as either positive or negative according to your opinion, i.e. it was a good or bad experience. We would very rarely say, 'It was a medium experience.' We often withhold a decision of like or dislike about a situation because the mind has not yet decided whether it brought pleasure or pain, so it says, 'Let me think about it.' Sooner or later it will make a judgment and store it in its negative or positive space within the atom of the cell.

The cortex stores memory and other brain cells and body organs store the opinions and feelings about each memory.

The second you look at something familiar, a memory surges forward and you judge whether what you see is bringing you the sensation of pleasure or not. Both the judgment and the feelings are working together, so they have a symbiotic relationship. You can see this in action by observing a memory: as it goes over the cortex, you will realise that it draws a feeling from you. This is the cells releasing your opinions, which are attached to the emotions. If you were to observe the memory and *feel* the feeling, then you are not only clearing the memory banks, you are also releasing the stored emotions from within the atom of the cells.

To find out how much time is actually spent caught up in the egoic mind ask yourself the following question: 'How much percentage of a day do you listen to your neutral or inner voice?' I have posed this question to many people and most have answered between the ranges of nought to twenty-five per cent. If you hear or feel the promptings of your inner voice, then how much of that percentage do you actually act upon? For example, I may listen to my inner voice or feelings ten per cent of the day, but I only act on five per cent of its guidance. The male and the female within are in a battle to get your attention and you are implementing the advice of these two, so your conditioning is actually leading ninety-five per cent of your daily life.

The mind exists in every cell and it is filled with the beliefs from the past. Every time you look at your partner, children, parents, friends, etc., you are seeing them as they were in the past and not as they are right in this moment. The second you glance at them, the whole past history you have shared with them comes forth from your cells. You remember every nuance, including times when your partner has complimented or hurt you. Each time you have a positive or negative experience with them, you adjust your beliefs, and your reaction to the person slightly shifts. You can sum up most relationships in two words, good or bad. You may say it has its good days and its bad days, but it is still based on opposites.

If you watched your thoughts as you look at your partner, you will see how all the judgments you have about him/her are flooding your mind. If you internalise these judgments, you will also notice how they are actually a reflection of you and all the issues in you which need to be faced. For example, you walk out of the supermarket behind your partner and you are struggling to carry the heavy shopping bags. He/she appears to be oblivious as he/she strides on in front whilst fishing for the car keys out of his/her pocket. You realise that he/she is not going to help you, which triggers old memories and this sets off a chain reaction in your atoms of all the times he/she has not supported you. The atoms begin to release the negative beliefs and irritation and anger surge forward. You fume in silence and do not say anything to him/her. Once you have calmed down the incident is stored back in the memory bank and the cells are filled with another negative experience of being unsupported, reinforcing your beliefs.

This process is happening constantly throughout a single day, but we are not aware of it, or we believe this way of being is 'normal' and until we face it, we will keep unconsciously drawing towards us repetitive incidents in order to release the suppressed energy. Once we have learnt from it we can let the pattern go and there is no need to attract it in again. The supermarket incident is showing you the example of how you are suppressing your needs and how you become irritated when people do not see that you need help. Maybe you have always come across as independent and capable, so those around you never realise that you require any physical support. This is the lesson your partner is teaching you. We need to communicate honestly with ourselves and with others, because we are expecting people to be mind readers and know what it is that we want.

Exercise: Write a list of the qualities that your ideal female would have and then do the same for your ideal male.
You may end up with something similar to the list below:

Female	Male
Nurturing	Strong
Creative	Decisive
Intuitive	Assertive
Attentive	Loving
Receptive	Dependable
Compassionate	Inspirational
Steadfast	Active
Reliable	Honest

Take a closer look at your list because what you are actually saying to yourself is that these qualities are what you want from your own inner male and female. You have been looking for someone external to bring these qualities to you. If you were to internalise them and live your life from them, then the desire for an external person to come and fix you or save you will fade away. In fact, these qualities are describing a fearless life. This is the foundation underpinning each quality.

The male and female within the atom are always trying to attract their opposite in order to make themselves complete. They are the other half of each other and the split is not their natural state, so they will always aim to heal themselves. Your external relationship is a reflection of this very process. The battle and separation between the male and the female will continue if we keep filling ourselves up with opinions and hold on to the past and all of its conditioning. There will be no inner peace if the egoic mind is active, because this is the false 'manufactured you' and not that which exists beyond this fickle movement between likes and dislikes.

This false you has many different masks which it greets each encounter with, and you only have to look at your own list of beliefs to know this. For example, one moment you maybe strong, the next you maybe angry or weepy, etc., in fact, you are trying on these different masks many times throughout any given day and under these masks are the images you portray to the world.

The Many Images

We often use the term 'to become whole', but what exactly are we really saying and what are these pieces which need to be unified? Maybe the atom is the reflection of the split within us and maybe the male, female and neutral have to come back together and function as one. At present we move between the three components within the atom and each one has a different way of expressing itself. The quickest way to know if you are fragmented and moving from one component to another, is to ask whether you change the way you act according to the person you are relating to.

This may be clearly obvious or very subtle. For example, you are stressed at work and your boss asks how you are, but instead of getting honest, you reply with a polite, 'Fine thankyou'. Your partner then calls you five minutes later and asks you the same question and you describe and moan about all of your work-related grievances. You may say your boss is not really interested in how you are and the question was only for show or courtesy, and if you answer honestly, it may reveal a weakness of not being able to cope with your job, so you pretend and you feel the boss is also pretending. You are in fact pasting over the truth with a fake frontage or image of coping. Over the period of your life you will meet hundreds of people whom you will communicate with, creating a similar amount of variations or images of you and others, but which image is the real you?

In order to understand how we create images and move from one image to another, we need to look at our beliefs and conditioning. For example, imagine thirty years ago two boys were born in a hospital in Jerusalem, one to Jewish parents and one to Muslim parents. By mistake the babies were switched and the Muslim was brought up as a Jew called Jonah and the Jew as a Muslim called Yoseph. Both were innocent and pure until they were taught about the history of their religious cultures and the hatred that wages between the two. Although they had never met, this sense of separation and antagonism towards each other's religious culture grew as they matured into adults. Twenty-nine years later they accidently meet in a jazz club in New York and because of their shared love of jazz they strike up a tentative friendship.

Also in New York, a man mysteriously lands on the Earth at the age of thirty-five with the ability to speak and understand any language. He has no memory, no past and no conditioning. Whilst walking past a jazz club, he hears the music and follows the sound into the club, where he sees two men sitting together at a table and so he asks to join them.

Jonah introduces himself as a Jew and Yoseph as a Muslim and they ask the man what religion he adheres to. The man replies that he does not understand the meaning of religion. Yoseph turns to Jonah and declares that he must be an atheist. The man asks what an atheist is. Jonah describes an atheist as a man who does not believe in God. The man asks what God is, and Jonah and Yoseph have a lively debate about what they believe God to be. They have now moved from their shared images of liking jazz into their religious images and they are trying to convince each other who has the right way to God. They start to raise their voices and blame each other about the war. Jonah is adamant about how the land of Israel is the Promised Land prophesied by Moses, but Yoseph argues that the Jews are stealing the lands from the Muslim tribes who lived there before the Jews came.

The man watches them with interest as they continue to talk over the top of each other without really listening to what is being said. Finally, they agree that because the man has no descendants, or history of being in Israel or any of the Islamic countries, it is best for him to become a Christian. Jonah tells the man how the Christians will accept someone who repents and becomes born again so that he does not have to go to hell when he dies. The man gets a little alarmed and asks what hell is. Yoseph describes how it is a place of evil where those who do not believe in God end up. The man exclaims that he does not want to go to such a place, so he asks how to become a Christian. Jonah points him in the direction of a church across the street and the man leaves the jazz club and enters the church. He is now on his way to creating an image through belief, conditioning and fear.

Diagram 2: Images in action.

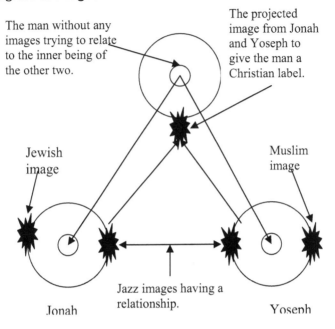

The man without any
images trying to relate
to the inner being of
the other two.

The projected
image from Jonah
and Yoseph to
give the man a
Christian label.

Jewish
image

Muslim
image

Jazz images having a
relationship.

Jonah

Yoseph

The circle or primeval atom of the man is pure and clear as he has no beliefs or conditioning and therefore no images. He communicates directly from the centre of his being as his real self, which is his neutral state or inner voice. He tries to connect with the centre of the other two, but their images are in the way, preventing them from having a proper relationship with him. The man does not know how to be anything else, so when they try to create an image of him and project the joint image into his being, he allows it in, because he now believes he must become something other than what he is in order for him to be accepted.

Jonah and Yoseph have a religious image and also a jazz image. Both jazz images are able to relate to each other, but the religious images stay out of the way due to the antagonism. Neither of these people are relating from their true essence. In truth only the images are actually having a relationship. Images are created from the past conditioning. The male and the female or ego within the atom, are projecting their positive and negative opinions as images onto the outer ring of the atom. Inside each human there will be hundreds of images stemming from beliefs on nationality, work ethics, lifestyle, racism, travel, etc., right through to personal judgments about strengths and weaknesses. We draw others towards us based on our images, and our positive friendships are based on all the good images we share, but our enemies or people we dislike are based on the fact that they bring us pain and clash with our beliefs.

Diagram 3: The male and female, or egoic mind, in the atom of the cell: projecting images based on judgments or opinions.

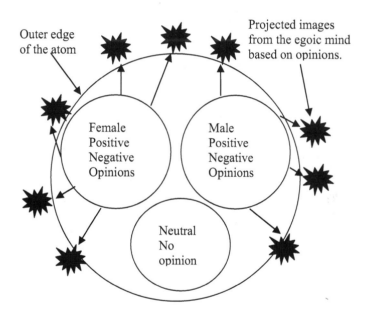

Outer edge of the atom

Projected images from the egoic mind based on opinions.

Female
Positive
Negative
Opinions

Male
Positive
Negative
Opinions

Neutral
No
opinion

We are all inter-relating with each other via our images. When you are with your mother, you act in a certain way, yet you will change your persona when you are with your father and the same goes for when you are with your partner, siblings, children, friends, etc. Each image is having a relationship with another image, but no-one is actually having a relationship with the real you.

If you look at diagram 3 you will notice that the neutral is very silent and not creating any image; it is just observing all the positive and negative interactions between the male and the female, so the inner voice is not based on any movement between the poles of opposites, but yet it must have a function.

If you were able to let go of a judgment, which is always based on like or dislike, all that would remain is fact, which is the truth of the situation. Therefore the inner voice is this fact and it can only act upon a fact and not upon the movement of like or dislike. For example, as a child you were physically abused and as an adult you believe the perpetrator is bad, or somehow you must have been bad and therefore you deserved it. If you see the person or what was done to you as bad, then you cannot move from the judgment and into the fact. You are stuck with the memories and the atoms are stuffed with negative beliefs. As a result you may have projected an image of yourself as a victim, or as someone who is aloof, etc.

If you begin to observe the person and the past situation by allowing the memories to move through you, the underlying facts will begin to reveal themselves. Now the inner voice is talking to you. What was done was an act of non-love, and the person was acting from their own conditioning. In the process they were putting pain and fear into your atoms and you stored it up as negative conditioning. The moment you see the truth of theirs, and your own, continued part in the drama of non-love, you can allow all the suppressed feelings in the atoms to come out.

In this way, the images created by your reaction to the above situation, can be released and you will create a space where peace can enter in. However, this will create a knock-on effect, and now you will need to deal with all the images that are created between those who share an opinion about you. For example, your mother will not only have judgments based on her personal experience with you, but she will have further views about you which she shares with your father, so another projection of 'who you are' is affecting your way of being. Your partner will share another image of you with your children, your friends and so forth, until you are completely bombarded with images of you which have absolutely nothing to do with the real you.

Diagram 4: Multiples of images in relationship.

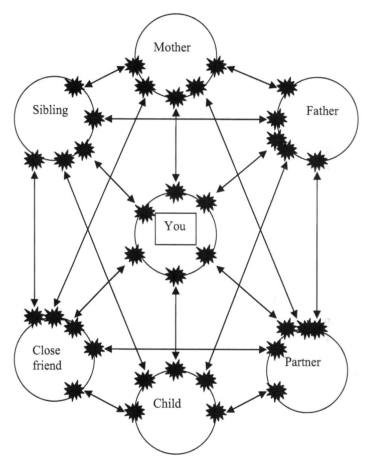

Each black explosion is an image you have of others and they have of you. This is an example of how each human is living their life, through an image which is created from a belief that stems from the past. In each moment you are living your life based on experiences from the past and there is no space to discover the new and the unknown.

The egoic mind is therefore the most active principle within the human mind and we do not know how to live without its images. For most people ninety-five per cent of their day is being played out through the illusionary-self. The very fact of seeing this truth and observing it in yourself releases the images. From this moment on, it is about the awareness of when you are being drawn back into relating to another's image, by getting caught up in the egoic mind's game of seeking pleasure versus avoiding/rejecting pain, of being a 'somebody' or a 'nobody'.

Most people fear dropping this egoic mind identity because they fear they will no longer be able to relate to others, and it may bring about a negative change in life circumstances. We are back to facing the fear of the unknown again, because only the egoic mind will question 'how to live' from this state of being. It wants to know the answer so it can feel safe enough to drop its images, but the images are the egoic mind, so it will resist because it believes it will die in the process of letting go. It is its own death which it fears the most, but you have been living this illusionary-self for most of your life, and it is who you have become. Most people are too afraid to move towards another way of being which does not rely on the acceptance of the many images. The individual personality each person expresses is shaped into being by the images created by the egoic mind. When you describe anyone's personality – another person's or your own – you are basing your knowledge only on images.

We actually deem our worth by the approval we receive from those around us; if we bring them pleasure, we are liked, but if we bring them pain, we are rejected. Some people go to the other extreme where they feel powerful if those around them are in fear of them, but none of these states is the true way of being because they are all egoic mind based. To live in a fearless state is to challenge the ego of others. At first they will try to continue to relate to you in the same old way, but when there is no longer any image from you to bounce off, their opinions will enter into a space which allows them to echo back and be shown for what they are, empty meaningless judgments.

Everything is relative and connected. For example, if you place a diseased cell under a microscope you will see how the shape of the cell is irregular and that the outer ring is being destroyed. The amount of projected images and the negative and positive beliefs in the atoms are creating an imbalance which allows bacteria in. We are slowly killing ourselves with the amount of garbage we carry, so what is the solution? If everyone in the world were to switch to ninety-five per cent of listening and taking action on the promptings of the inner voice, what kind of world would we create? There would be very little egoic mind, illness, few images or games of intent using manipulation, seduction and parasitic behaviour. So why can't the human race do it? We all know this world needs a massive transformation in order to continue to survive, but most people do not realise that the power for this change is within them.

If the neutral or inner voice spoke to the inner voice of another without any block or distortion, would this be love and truth in motion? What would it be like to have a relationship without all the illusion and pretence? If you had no images would you still hide your vulnerability and innocence? Would other people's meaningless judgments of you really matter or would you not even acknowledge what is said because you know of its illusion?

The images your egoic mind have created have no relation to the real you at all, as they are dual in nature. When an image from you is relating to the image in another, the relationship will be based on illusion and it will have aspects of conflict in it. If you meet a person who has no egoic mind, then how can an egoic mind relate to a non-egoic mind? Egoic mind has within it positive and negative, non-egoic mind does not, so it cannot relate. A person who lives predominantly from their egoic mind will either walk away, having reinforced their image of you, or they will drop all their conditioning. It is impossible to put a split material atom into an immaterial whole atom. It is the same with the egoic mind; it cannot live or relate to non-egoic mind.

To carry on in the same vein of self-destruction is no longer an option for humanity and this planet. The truth is: you are not who you have become. The egoic mind is the make-up of all of your past conditioning and it creates images based on its opinions of like and dislike, which is your personality in action, but you are more than this. You are the intelligence of the eternal creator, which resides in its unmanifest, infinite silent space. This is the neutral or inner voice that resides in every atom of your body, and this voice speaks to you in each moment, but you continually cover it over with the mind, which wants the dramas from living in opposites.

This chapter may have shown you how to separate the truth from the illusion within yourself, but how are you going to face the fear which stops you from taking the action needed in order to be free?

Chapter 6

Why am I in Pain?

What is a person doing, or what have they done, to create the feeling of separateness between them and me? If it is their anger, their jealousy, their pride, or whatever emotion is driving them to hurt me, surely the same emotion must be inside me. I recognise how we have all got fear, anger, jealousy and desire. In some people it is more apparent and maybe their jealousy is more highlighted or maybe it is their fear which is motivating them. Everyone is affected by emotion, so we are not different, and we are all trying to find a way through the suffering of these emotions, whether we admit it or not.

Fear Begins at the First Point of Pain

A newborn baby reacts when it feels physically uncomfortable, i.e. hungry, hot, cold, wet, etc. This is a natural survival instinct, but the first point of pain is the stopping point in a child's life from when they first encounter fear through an act of non-love from another. The emotional reaction from the child at this point is paramount to how the person will deal with pain and fear for the rest of his or her daily life until they face and release this pain.

This point of shock at the experience of non-love is the very beginning of memory. Emotion is energy in movement, but a shock creates a stopping point of this natural flow. If it does not quickly recover, it no longer flows and it becomes blocked and ultimately stagnant. If we do not deal with this shock and continue to add more emotions on top of it by suppressing our truth and creativity, we allow fear to enter in and become the driving force behind thought. The journey of how to reject future pain, and desire only pleasure, has begun.

Before this initial encounter with fear, the child does not have any mental knowledge of the opposites existing within his or her world, because a child who has not experienced fear, very rarely thinks about yesterday or tomorrow, as they live solely for the moment. From the point of being in a situation which lacks love, they begin to remember life as incidents based on pleasure and pain. The child has now become aware of not only fact-based language, but also language which holds emotion. For example, before knowing fear a child will relate to the word 'dog' as a descriptive fact. When this word is spoken the child will accept its description without any emotion, but if the child is licked or bitten by a dog, the word 'dog' now has a pleasant or terrifying feeling attached to it. The word is no longer just a descriptive fact, but a link to a point of pleasure or pain, which is stored as a happy or fearful memory.

Fear is therefore intricately woven with mind and memory. If you were to travel back in your mind from your current age to your conception, you will find a key memory of where you first ever felt pain and therefore fear. At this point of pain you will have reacted emotionally. For example, a woman looks back over her life and finds how her first memory of pain occurred when she was three. She remembers sitting at the kitchen table when she accidently drops her cup and spills the drink all over the floor. In response, her mother shouts at her, slaps her legs and makes her cry. Her immediate reaction to the pain is to feel helpless, bad and rejected, which is non-love.

From this incident, the woman realises how her reaction to the pain of not being loved has since shaped her life. Each time a situation occurred she would try to control it by aiming to make the outcome of any circumstance nice, which kept those closest to her happy, thus avoiding this experience of non-love from ever happening again. She has been actually living from a belief that to upset people will bring them and her pain, and the feelings of being helpless, bad and rejected. The *fear* of giving and receiving non-love is what is driving her.

Every human has this first point of pain within them and they have been living their life from the reaction it created which may include feelings of rejection, anger, helplessness, frustration, lack of worth and all the rest of the many labels of pain that is intimately mingled with fear. From this very first experience of non-love we created a pivotal point which set the foundations of our future life. In truth, very few people have moved beyond this stage, as most points of pain occur between conception and seven, so virtually the entire world population is still stuck in childhood.

There has been much written about this stuck inner child and how we have prevented it from expressing itself. What we clearly understand is that a large portion of the real us has been shut down, ignored or left behind. We have not moved from this crucial time in childhood which created a shock to the system, and we have since been living a very small potential of our life's possibilities.

A moment after we experienced this act of non-love we subconsciously not only rejected and separated the inner male and the female within the atom, but we also denied the inner voice or the real us. We did this because there was an instant recognition of our humanness, and we realised that the inner female was rendered as helpless in the situation, the inner male was in shock and did not know how to handle the experience, and we did not believe that the inner voice could save us.

From this moment, in order to protect ourselves from any further incidents of pain, we now do one of two things.

1. We allow the inner male to rise up into the mind, where intellectual and analytical pursuits become more important, and we suffocate the voice of the inner female, as the inner male now perceives her as helpless and in need of protection.

2. The inner female suppresses the inner male as it did not protect her, and we become a submissive external female or male who is always searching for safety with an air of victimisation. The inner female believes she can no longer rely on the inner male to protect her.

This first point of pain actually causes us to enter into either the male or the female side of our brain, which causes us to shift our energy into one side of our body. The right side of the body is predominantly male and the left is female. By living mainly in one side we subconsciously deplete energy from the organs that reside there and we control and suppress their expression. The female doubts the ability of the male to protect her, as she never knows when it is going to switch from being nice to using or abusing her in some capacity, so she can become apathetic and weak. The male sees the female as too feeble to handle circumstances when acts of non-love are taking place, so he can become aggressive and frustrated.

If this is happening internally, then it is also happening externally. If you are a female, you will have an element of distrust towards the male person in your life, and if you are a male, you will have a belief in the weakness of the females around you. Ultimately, both have a distrust of each other and because the inner voice has been pushed out of the equation as the non-saviour, each person will be living their daily life by using ninety-five per cent of their mind in order to avoid, or be prepared for, the suffering and the acts of non-love which are going to occur.

This leads us to a very important question: why, if there is such a thing as God, who is supposedly ultimate love, how can acts of suffering occur in the first place? Many people have asked why God does not save humanity from starvation, decay, disease, atrocities from nature, terrorism and accidents, etc. When this question has been put before the institutions of religion, some have replied that we have to suffer for the sins of others. But is this an act of love? Would an all-loving God say, 'Go and suffer from the acts of rape, murder, starvation, loss, and pain in order to set your brother free and prove your worth'? This answer to such a deep and probing question is only an excuse for more suffering. There is something else going on here, and we have been filled up with utter rubbish whose only job is to stop us from looking deeper at the issue.

There is another important question which has been put at the door of the Christian religion: why did God allow his only Son to be killed on the cross, because if he were that powerful, surely God would have shown himself and saved him? Maybe what we are really asking is: if the inner voice of Jesus did not save him from the suffering on the cross, then neither can our inner voice help us, so what's the point in following it? This is a fabulous argument for the egoic mind to ask the inner voice.

The egoic mind believes it has the upper hand over the inner voice and it has become very powerful. It lives in total rejection of the inner voice, which is love, as it believes it to be powerless against the negativity which prowls upon this planet. The ego will tell you that to follow the guidance of this inner voice is dangerous, as it will lead you into unknown territory, which may result in further suffering. So you continue to live in fear of the unknown future, and the only way through this mire of fear, is to face the issues which you are running from.

The inner voice is therefore the only tool you have which can take you through the fear. The egoic mind will try to keep you in it, but the inner voice will show you a path to freedom. By agreeing to undertake this inner journey of facing the illusionary self you have created, you will be at the mercy of the egoic mind. This will play out in your internal battles and also through the changes that will occur in your external life, which may not at first appear to be beneficial. This journey will lead to the death of your egoic mind and it will try to crucify you as you move away from the illusions of fear. It will create upheaval and even threaten you with the loss of material possessions, etc., but you are going to have to let go and trust something that is not known to you or seen by the physical eyes. It is this very trusting which will make you vulnerable as you face the very fears of doubt and helplessness which keep the male and female separated within the atom.

If we look at the biblical life of Jesus we can see how he challenged the egoic mind, doctrine and society, which revealed the workings of opposites in action. Two thousand years on and the message still remains the same. It may appear to the human mind that he was not physically saved from his death, but those who followed him wrote about his life declared how he was the embodiment of love, so maybe in his own inner world, his inner voice did save him, but not as a physical act, which is how the mind believes it should have been done.

The egregore of total mind works on the principles of 'divide and rule'. Whenever you separate yourself from another by seeing yourself as 'you' and the other as 'them' you are in fact reacting from your own individual egoic mind. The belief that this separation is going to protect you from all that is 'bad' is an illusion. The emotional reaction at the first point of pain is what keeps this separation confined within a set of walls and these walls are governed by fear.

Living in a Box

Each human has therefore created a self-made box, which has limited the expression of the true self. All of our opinions, conditioning and images communicate themselves through the walls of this box and now everything we think, say and do is tainted with fear. It is as though every single primeval atom in the body is trapped in this small confined space, and our relationships from this point are based on our emotional reactions which are trying to protect us from feeling any pain.

The distrust, which exists between the male and the female, keeps them separated and they are at war, competing with each other as they throw their opinions through the walls of the box. The neutral, which is the inner voice, continues to go unheard. It cannot break through the walls, because love cannot travel through fear, only fear can move through fear.

Exercise: The Box: Without looking at diagram 5 overleaf:

1. Draw a box.

2. Place one door and two windows on the outer walls of the box, similar to an architectural layout, i.e.

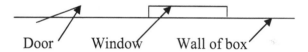

Door   Window   Wall of box

3. Draw a circle in the box that touches each wall.

4. On the edges of this circle draw your images as seen in diagram 3.

5. Inside this circle feel where the man needs to be and draw him in stickman form.

6. Now feel where the female needs to be placed and draw her in the stickman form.

7. Finally, using feeling again, draw another circle to represent the inner voice and place it within the larger circle in the box.

Most people will draw a box similar to diagram 5 below.

Diagram 5: The box

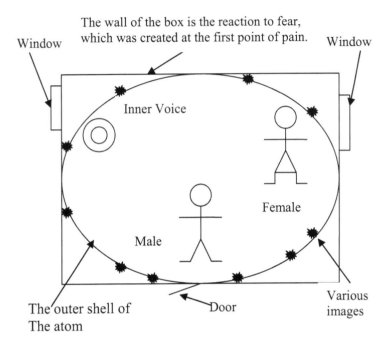

The wall of the box is the reaction to fear, which was created at the first point of pain.

Window

Window

Inner Voice

Female

Male

The outer shell of
The atom

Door

Various
images

The male is usually near the door or very central within the box. This shows how most people have a very active and protective male which is more prominent than their inner female. In order for the female to get out of the box she has to confront and pass through the male, which will create an inner battle of wills. This is the conditioned opinions of your mother and father that bubble up in your mind. You will usually hear them in your own voice and they are mostly conflictive about making decisions on how you should act.

If the female is allowing the male to be the dominant one, but you have still drawn a window near her, then you are permitting her to have a view of what is outside the box. On rare occasions she may be allowed to express an opinion, but the male will still hold onto the belief that she is too helpless to deal with making life decisions, which are usually based on the need for some form of security. People often draw the female smaller than the male, which can mean that a large proportion of the person's emotions are suppressed, allowing anger to be the dominant emotion. Underneath anger you will always find grief and below this lies the initial shock which was created at the first experience of fear or non-love.

The inner voice is usually in a corner, some give it a window, which means they hear the inner voice, but they do not take the necessary action. If it is without a window and smaller than the male and the female, then the person is far removed from their true spiritual heritage. The male is the representative of the mind, the female of the emotions and the neutral is the personal contact with the creator of life, but most people are living predominantly in their male energy only and therefore they are mainly living an intellectual life.

Each time the male or the female is prodded by an external factor, it chooses its opinion from its negative and positive beliefs and projects them through the walls of the box, adding to it the reaction to fear from the very first point of pain. This whole process of memory, which has pain or pleasure attached to it, moving through the walls of fear and being expressed in the daily life of a person, is what keeps the egoic mind intact.

The Nemesis

Every human you meet will be relating to you from this process of their egoic mind. This means you are constantly relating from box-to-box and what comes through the walls of the box, which is image-to-image. The only way you can break down the walls of your box is to find your first point of pain and feel your emotional reaction to the experience and understand how you have lived your life from this point. It is this very realisation of yourself which causes the walls to crumble. For example, the woman who was slapped by her mother when she was three is constantly trying to keep her world safe and happy. This causes her to be obedient to the will of others in order to keep the peace.

At the time of her first point of pain the female within her felt helpless, as there was no-one there to save her and she did not know how to deal with her situation. The male within her rose up into the intellect and has since taken on the role of protector by keeping her out of difficult situations and putting her into secure environments, creating a wall around her. This should logically work, but problems occur when she relates to other human beings who also have their first point of pain in a form of a box and images. She could hide herself away, but only through relating can she really solve the problem of her egoic mind. One particular person who pushes her buttons of fear is her boss, whose own first point of pain brought up the reaction of anger and this is how he is reacting to the world around him.

Each time they meet the boss demands through his anger and the woman immediately reacts with obedience, as she is trying to keep herself safe. Both of them are using their inner males to deal with the situation, but the boss has an aggressive male which is overpowering her protective male and reducing it to what it fears the most, which is being female and helpless. The nemesis is therefore a person who is highlighting the walls of your box and they are showing you what needs to be healed within your being. You may know this nemesis as your enemy or the most difficult person in your life that you have to cope with.

Once you realise how you have been reacting to people you will want to find a way to deal with it. The very fact of seeing yourself reacting from a fear-based position is all that is needed to begin with, as now you can take a different route from the road of fear. If the woman in question turned to her boss and said, 'You are making me feel like a victim', then she has only confirmed what he is doing and she has not solved the problem. When he hears her fear the boss will do one of two things: he will either continue in the same vein, or temporarily cool his temper, but this is not actually healing his anger or getting to the root of his fear. Subconsciously, he wants people to feel threatened by him because then he is not open to being hurt or abused. He is trying to make sure he never has to experience the circumstances of his first point of pain ever again.

104

The woman is also trying to avoid an experience of her first point of pain by controlling her environment and making secure avenues to retreat into.

Both of them are living from their male energy whilst protecting the inner female from abuse. If either of them switches into the energy of their inner female they will feel vulnerable and insecure. Moving from one energy to its opposite is not the solution either, as each of the energies hold their own negative and positive beliefs, so balance cannot be found because beliefs separate one human from another. They could listen to their inner voice, which will guide them, but the walls of the box are still intact, so they will hear the inner voice, but they will be too afraid to take the necessary action.

It only takes one person to set off a chain reaction of change and this can be done by asking one of two questions which challenge your actions and those of other people:

1. Why did you do that?

2. Why did I do that?

When someone puts you down with a verbal judgment and you respond with, 'Why did you do that?' what will happen? If you put question 2 to yourself after you have been judgmental to someone else, what will happen to you? Immediately it makes you stop and look at what lies behind the judgment. If you keep looking you will find that fear was the root cause of your thoughts, words and action.

If you go back to your first point of pain you will find that the only real question you have for the person who brought forth the experience of non-love is, 'Why did you do that?'. If you continue to look across the span of your life you will also see all the times you have wanted to ask that question of another and of yourself. When you actually break down the meaning of the sentence, what you are really asking is, 'Why did you not love me?', and each time you have reacted from your images and your walls, you are asking yourself, 'Why did I not love you?'

Using the example of the woman and her boss: the next time he approaches her with his angry brusque manner, rather than reacting from her walls of fear, she can ask him, 'Why did you do that?' The second these words leave her lips she is going to have to feel the fear that will be churning in her gut, and all of the habitual reactions which have governed her life to this point will no longer be speaking for her. This means she has moved out of behaving according to her victim image and stepped into the unknown, challenging fear itself. All of her feelings of helplessness and insecurity will rise up to be felt, and the moment will become very vivid to her because she does not know how he will react. Maybe she will lose her job, or he could become more violent as his own fears are being challenged, but maybe, just maybe, he might pause for a moment and go within himself and ask himself why he is treating her this way. If he does not accept the challenge, but she continues to face her walls of fear in every situation, her life circumstances will change and she will no longer need him as a nemesis in her life.

The first step to facing the patterns which have held you as a prisoner in your box will take courage, because you are going to have to feel the fear that goes with expressing yourself honestly. All the times you said 'what if' or 'I should' or 'I shouldn't' will flit across your mind. By facing and challenging the fact that the situation is a non-loving one, will bring all your fears and conditioning to the forefront. Try it and find out for yourself what will happen.

One Cell Reflects the Whole of You

Each cell within the body carries with it all the information of your life, which includes your thoughts, emotions, actions, fears and desires. Before a cell dies a natural death it passes this information onto a new cell, so your body reflects the sum total of your life. A diseased cell therefore passes on the disease to another cell and so forth. The irregularity of shape which occurs in a diseased cell is when the outer membrane of the cell has become toxic. It has changed from a pure state to an impure state, but what makes this occur and why?

When a person suppresses the natural expression of their real self, which is living without fear, they begin to fill up the atoms within the cells with this non-expressed energy. After many years of this constant holding back, the cells become clogged and the system begins to become sluggish, and congested. We may experience early signs of a problem in the body through various aches and pains etc., but if the message is ignored, then serious illness begins to take shape in the cells.

If you watch a flower from bud to decay you will notice how it gives off different smells throughout its life span. At the point of bloom it can be very pleasant to the senses, but as it declines it becomes acidic. Decay has a very close relationship with acidic states. The body has a natural pH balance of approx 7.4. This is calculated by measuring the pH samples of saliva and urine taken at the same time, added together and divided by two. If the pH gets below 7.0 the body is beginning to turn acidic, which means that harmful bacteria found in food, water and air, can now enter into the cells and begin the process of decay. Bacteria can only survive in acidic conditions, so a healthy person is slightly alkaline, which protects them from disease.

Most newborn babies born to healthy mothers are slightly alkaline and if they are breastfed by a mother who is eating a balanced diet, then they can create a strong immune system. If the mother's breast milk is slightly acidic, the baby will be prone to colds and viruses. If the baby is kept at a slightly alkaline state through healthy breast milk, but is then put on solids and fed more acidic foods, the cells will begin to open up to the entry of bacteria.

In our modern world we are always trying to become more male and the food we eat reflects this in motion. All meats, fast food, alcohol, etc., are acid-forming and male in nature, so the majority of us are open to being invaded by micro-organisms, which will be detrimental to our health. The same applies to a

107

person who goes to the other extreme and eats only a female alkali-forming diet of raw fruit and raw vegetables.

When you eat too many male products you are pushing out the female within the cell and the effect is similar to that of the exploding atom. Over time your body will swell and expand as you become more male and your heart will feel the pressure building up as the arteries harden, until eventually a heart attack, aneurism or cancer of the colon occurs. A body which lives on extreme female foods will begin to implode, as there is no male to balance it, so illnesses such as anorexia, bulimia and brain spasms can manifest.

Subconsciously, we often use our diet to keep us living in one side of either the male or the female energy. A balanced daily diet of seventy-five per cent alkali-forming foods and twenty-five percent acid-forming foods will keep the pH at healthy levels. If you have been predominantly living in either the male or the female side of your energy, this balanced diet will throw you into a period of deep cathartic healing. The bacteria, which are living in your cells and feeding off your suppressed issues, will react to the new regime and you may experience cravings, headaches, nausea, irritation, anger and weepiness as you transform the state of your cells.

Your egoic mind lives in every atom within the cells of your body, as do the images you hold about yourself and others. It is these which have become toxic and created a space for bacteria to enter in. When people make a judgment about you and project that judgment onto you, it becomes an image in the atom, affecting the cells and these very judgments are the invading bacteria. They can only survive in your cells if there is a weakness, which is fear. A person, who has let go of their egoic mind and all the images they have created about, or accepted from another, has nothing in the cells which would allow invading bacteria to stick to. It is an empty space, so bacteria travel straight on through, as there is no stopping place.

The mind is a tool needed to store the memory of how to function chronologically on this planet. Once the first point of fear entered in, mind took on the role of protector, and the central 'I' or egoic mind was born. This illusionary-self now moved between the opposite poles of pleasure and pain, based on desire, and opinions between like and dislike were created and became stored in the cells, forming numerous images. These preferences were expressed externally, giving a person an individual personality.

A healthy cell therefore reflects the process of a cortex which allows the energy of memory, thought and fear to pass over it without reacting to it. Clear the atomic structure of the brain by observing your desires, your thoughts and their movement between the past and the future and you will clear the trillions of atoms within a single cell, or visa versa; clear the atoms within the cells by being aware of your reaction to fear, dropping your images, observing your judgments and by eating a balanced diet, and this will throw the brain into the same process.

The Truth Versus Your Truth

The only constant you can rely on whilst going through this process of clearing the self is the inner voice, but many people do not know how to find it or recognise it. When a person first starts to listen out for the inner guidance they meet various voices within the mind which are all vying to be heard. As mentioned in part one, when you were born you were an empty vessel and the role models around you taught you how to think in language, but you were never taught how to feel. This was already a natural movement inside of you, so the inner voice communicated with you through your feelings, but problems occurred because people also taught you how to override your feelings by using your mind. This external teaching of utilising the mind as an authority has now been internalised and your inner mind continues to show you how to override your feelings.

What your mind sees as the truth is actually based on the foundations of your opinions and therefore it is not reliable. *The truth*, which is related to you through the inner voice, is based on the whole picture as a fact. Truth has no emotion, no likes and no dislikes attached to it, and it is immovable, whereas opinions are subject to change. If you are looking at something from the opinions held in the female aspect of your atom within the cell, you will see it one way, and if you switch into the male aspect, you will see it in its opposite, but the inner voice sees it as it is, with all the components laid bare. To find out how you can access the inner voice, the following exercise is a fantastic example of showing you a way through the myriad of voices.

Exercise: The inner voice. Place three chairs in a line all facing the same way.

Stand with your back to the chairs and describe out loud the basics of a problem you currently have. If you are a female sit in the chair on your left, which is your inner female and speak out loud about what she feels about the problem. If you are a male, sit on the chair to your right and describe what your male thinks about the problem.

Once you have finished talking, switch from the female chair to the male chair and vice versa for the male. Describe again what each feels and thinks about the problem. Now sit in the middle chair and let your inner voice have its say.

You will find all three have something different to say. The female usually describes the fear of taking action or causing others pain, the male often talks about rejection, anger and indecisiveness and the inner voice speaks without any fear or anger, and is the one who describes exactly what needs to be done to solve the problem.

Once you get used to doing this exercise with the three chairs, you can actually internalise it by asking the question inwardly, and then listening for the response of the male, female and inner voice. You will soon realise how the decisions made by the male and female are based upon your past conditioning and fears, and you will see clearly how the inner voice bases its information on facts. Each time you follow the impulse to operate from the decisions of your inner male and female, which is not in agreement with your inner voice, you are actually moving your energy into one or the other side of your body. This causes you to act from illusion and become imbalanced.

All those voices inside of your head that are competing for your attention are the opinions from your inner male and female, which is the egoic mind. The quiet voice or feeling, which is not competing for your attention, but is observing and communicating facts to you, is the inner voice. This is the difference between *the truth* and *your truth*. To follow these facts is to trust and when you trust, you let go of the outcome. The inner voice only has one real message that it relays to you as part of the fact, and that is to let go and surrender.

Attachment to Outcomes

The egoic mind becomes attached to an outcome because it is always protecting itself from painful experiences, so it always wants to make sure that what it is doing will end in pleasure and success. The moment you are inspired by your inner voice to do something new or take action, you immediately want to know the end result. If you cannot see the end result, then your mind begins to analyse and assess all the possible problems you are going to meet with, and it starts to solve these problems before you have even taken the first step.

The egoic mind is terrified of the unknown because it may bring you an experience of pain. Look across your life and you will see how you have an end goal for everything, from how a relationship should be, to how your home, your car, your job, or the success of your children, should be, etc. If you don't achieve these goals, you just change the goal posts and keep striving for another satisfactory result. You may even have lists of how you are going to obtain these goals, because you think that if you achieve them, then bingo, your life will finally be happy.

This is the real battle between the inner voice and the egoic mind, because if you follow the inner voice it is going to take you into unknown areas and you cannot protect yourself where everything is unfamiliar, so you feel out of control and lost. The egoic mind strives for safety, as it has projected an end result and figured out steps of how to get there. What your egoic mind desires may not be beneficial for your real self, but it does not matter because your ego is safe. This conflict your ego has with the inner voice will make you feel uncomfortable. Some mornings you may wake up questioning what you are doing with your life, but the ego takes control of your thoughts again and before you know it, bam, you forget about that gnawing ache inside and once more you are off on your safe path.

This is why we are in pain, because the majority of us are living ninety-five per cent of our daily life from the point of the egoic mind. There are some people who can listen and take action on a large percentage of their inner voice, but there are very few who listen and act upon ninety-five per cent or more. This illusionary-self does not know, or even have a relationship with the true self; instead, it keeps it covered over with fear. We are truly frightened of the unknown and we grasp at what we believe will bring us security and a place to be safe from feeling any abuse or pain, but there is no external safe place, because the material is always changing and moving. The only place to reside safely is with the inner voice, because it knows how to chart these waters of impermanence.

Many people say we have free will or choice, but do we really? The egoic mind has opposites within it, so when listening to it you do have a choice between pleasure and pain. The inner voice however, has no separation in it, so when listening to it you see the truth as it is. The action you take upon this truth is not formed out of choice, but comes from love. This stunning and amazing energy has its own path to follow. You can ride with it or not.

The journey of a life which listens to the inner voice is a journey with the true self, which is love. A life spent listening to the egoic mind is a movement into non-love, based on fear, conditioning and desire. This path will lead the individual into a battle of trying to become a 'somebody' rather than a 'nobody', resulting in a huge sense of loneliness and separation.

Chapter 7

The Power of the Individual Mind

The human mind has the power to create or destroy. Each individual upon the Earth is either adding to the destructive element or the creative element. What we destroy or create affects not only ourselves, but also everything on this planet. The fate of humanity lies inside of you. How much do you love life?

Like Attracts Like

The mind is a very powerful tool and left unchecked it acts autonomously, becoming egoic and self-centred in nature. It uses your thoughts, which are based on fear and the past, and it blocks the flow of the inner voice within. Humans have made the egoic mind the central focus for living, giving it the freedom to create confusion and chaos in the world. If you look around the globe, all the suffering you see is created by individual egoic minds joining together to form huge egregores, which carry out the desires of the collected thoughts. If every human dropped the constant movement between the opposites in the mind and the striving to become, the world would reach a state of peace. Humans would stop killing humans, animals and nature, and this would have a knock-on effect and nature would stop killing nature.

Can you imagine a world without the constant suffering? What would be left for the newspapers and the T.V to report about? What would happen to the film and literary industries? Would children's books still have a good and bad theme running through them? How would the pharmaceutical companies make billions if people rarely got sick, or if they did get sick they turned to plants from nature to heal themselves? If love was the predominant emotion on this planet, everything would have to change. Love attracts to itself only love and fear attracts fear. The current state of your life is showing you the energy you are attracting to yourself, because like a magnet, you can only draw in what is similar to that which you are giving expression to.

The positive push and the negative pull action between the male and the female within the atom are creating a constant swinging motion. Therefore, whatever you are trying to reject and keep out of your life by pushing it away, will in actual fact draw it in. If you think negative thoughts, you will attract similar thoughts to you from the negative energy which exists in the ether that surrounds you.

So-called 'positive thinking' is not the answer either. The whole movement of therapeutic mind techniques, which teach you to have positive affirming thoughts in order to attract more positive energy towards you, are still mind-based. This process works well for a short period of time before your negative thoughts, which you are rejecting and suppressing, begin to bubble up and re-surface again. Neuro Linguistic Programming (NLP) and similar mind techniques are therefore only a plaster over a deep wound.

The same applies to the various meditation systems. The mind is using itself to concentrate on a fixed point in order to attain peace, or to experience spiritual ecstasy, but this is still within the confines of mind and therefore it is illusionary. You have not gone beyond mind, you have just reached the highest point of positive mind, but it is still mind, which is a material entity. It is the same principle as giving a naughty child a toy to play with. It keeps the child focused on the toy and entertained for a while, but the root of the naughtiness is still there. The toy has not solved the problem; it has only temporarily alleviated it.

There is much written about the positive results of using meditation to ease stress levels or of learning from a supposed master or guru, on how to subdue the ego, but for the normal human being who has a nine-to-five job, with a family, a mortgage and expectations to meet, how can they get free from this trap of the egoic mind? Most people are not even aware of how their egoic mind is in control of their life, so they continue in this meaningless mind-based life in naivety and only question their existence when things go wrong. Each individual has the power to change their external world, but the root cause of it lies within, so the only way to get free is to start from within. It would be easier to suppress the egoic mind and channel it into a point of focus, but this would only create more confusion, as, eventually, suppressed thoughts emerge, so it is better to look closely at one's own egoic mind in order to understand it and set it free.

Thought Projection

We have discussed how the memory banks surround the cortex and how thoughts float over the cortex, which causes it to reach up and latch itself to the thought and give it energy. If we were to just observe the passing thoughts, we will notice how they move through the mind and then disperse. By giving them attention, we give them energy, and as a result the thought forms become animated and expansive. These thought forms now have the power to move from your mental energy field and travel to wherever the content directs it. To a person who is not aware, this process occurs thousands of times a day, and they are autonomously sending energy to other people and places in every moment. This energy greatly affects the subject it is being directed to.

A person who is aware takes great care in the observation of their thoughts and any projections that may occur from an emotional reaction to a situation. They are often very sensitive to the energies that surround them, and because of their ability to observe and listen they can often take on too much energy from those around them. Therefore, it is important to recognise when you have had enough of a social situation and then have the courage to remove yourself from further projections and energetic displacements from others.

The most damaging thoughts are those which set out to destroy the peace of another person through jealousy, envy, judgment and obsession. For example, diagram 6 below is showing a heart-to-heart relationship between two people who have worked on their minds and egos and dealt with the duality which resides within them. We shall call them John and Sally. The third person has no self-knowledge and still lives within the confines of his illusionary self. We shall call him James.

Diagram 6: Thought Projection

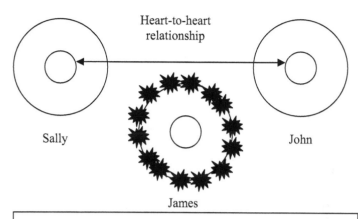

Heart-to-heart
relationship

Sally

John

James

> ✳ = The various polluted and disturbed images of James.
> Both Sally and John have let go of their conditioning
> and no longer create images of themselves and others.

James meets Sally at a weekend business conference and he immediately feels a strong connection to her. His first impulse is that the sight of her brings him pleasure and he starts to desire her and think sexual thoughts about her. These thoughts get stronger as the weekend progresses and because she is not reacting to him, he starts to create more perverted thoughts and distortion. He begins to become obsessed and he tries to manoeuvre situations around him so he can be near her. Sally starts to feel uncomfortable around him and she knows what he is doing with his thoughts. A constant influx of images are flooding the space in her cells and although she does not get caught up in them and allows them to pass through her, the weight from the build-up of mass thought and their content of contamination is draining her and she is beginning to weaken and tire. She is losing her vitality as it is now being used to deal with the constant projections from James.

At the end of the weekend they leave the convention, but he continues to be obsessed with her and his thinking does not stop. After a few weeks Sally is now very worn down by the projections and her energy is seriously depleted. The constant bombardment of filth is affecting her sleep and she no longer radiates her peace out into the world. The irritation of not being at peace causes her to find fault with John who is trying to maintain the equilibrium between them, but she is now assaulting his energy with petty accusations and the love they share is diminishing.

John can no longer take the upset to his system as it is causing him to re-create an egoic mind, which is reacting through defence, so he asks for them both to stop everything and talk about what happened at the convention.

It is vital at this point that they totally listen to each other without the mind influencing the conversation with its blame and judgments. So, to understand the problem in its entirety, they discuss the events in an emotionally detached and factual way. They soon realise that the distortion stems from James, but they still cannot stop his thoughts from entering Sally's personal space.

Day after day the onslaught continues and even though they are aware of his projections, they cannot prevent it from also affecting their children, and the pollution is spreading throughout the family. Small disturbances, which they would not normally draw towards them, start to happen, because the distortion projected from James now sits as backlogged energy in their cells and it is attracting similar energy to it, so more distortion is entering into their lives.

One single person is affecting the lives of many, but what can Sally and John do about it? They decide to contact James and tell him about the chaos his thoughts are creating and ask him why he is doing it. James responds with arrogance and still continues with his onslaught. It was only his image that listened to them, and because his thoughts bring him pleasure, he does not want to give them up. Diagram 7 shows this occurring.

Diagram 7: The effects of Thought Projection.

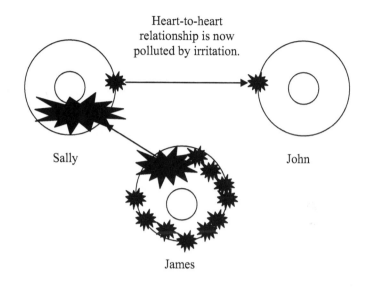

Heart-to-heart
relationship is now
polluted by irritation.

Sally

John

James

> James is creating chaos with his thoughts and disturbing the love
> between Sally and John. As a result of the pollution Sally is now
> projecting irritation and anger onto John and the flow of love is
> being blocked.

The only thing John and Sally can do is to keep themselves as
clear as possible. They do this by being open and honest with
each other, spending as much time in nature as they can, having
cold showers as a way of magnetically pulling the negativity
from their energy, and using the mind to visualise mirrors facing
James.

Over time James loses interest in Sally and he finds another
person to become obsessed with. His thoughts are no longer
being projected onto Sally, but now another person is feeling all
the distortion and pollution. If this person is not self-aware or
does not know how to deal with this type of energy they can
become drained, until eventually they fall ill. Some people do
not mind being obsessed over, they feel that to be adored is
some sort of compliment and so they are de-sensitised to the
damage which is being done to them. They do not relate the

tiredness and illness to the projected thoughts from another. A person who is living a life beyond the mind and ego is love in motion. This love immediately feels when an act of non-love occurs, but a person who is already filled with pollution will not notice more pollution because it is no different from what is already there.

There are limits to the amount of pollution the human body can endure. The judgments you have about yourself and the thought projections from others are actually shortening your life. You are also affecting the life of those people you think about. When you project your opinions, beliefs and desires into someone else's system, then know how they will have to spend a large amount of energy to clean up what really belongs to you. Ultimately, it will start to seep into the cells and into the organs, poisoning the life-giving essence.

This is what has been happening to the individual human being since time immemorial. There are pure loving beings on this planet and it only takes one person to project distorted thoughts into their being and block them from loving. We believe it is OK to think these thoughts and we never question where the thoughts go, or how we are affecting another human being with our judgments, opinions and desires.

Dumping Your Baggage

Thought projection not only affects the energy of other life-forms, but it also affects inert objects and the ether or air of this planet. Buildings are a great example of how thought energy builds up within a set of walls. You only have to step into a hospital, an old people's home or a nightclub to get a feel of what is being thought about there. When a person walks into a public place and continues to think via their conditioning, they are dumping this energy into the space. Once it hits the ether, it begins to gyrate towards other like-minded thoughts that are already there. For example, the intensive care unit in a hospital holds denser energy than the delivery suite. They can even be on the same floor, but one may have more energy focused on the fear of death and the other on the excitement of new life.

The same principle applies to objects. Through repeated use or familiarity with an object, the owner will leave an imprint of their energy on it. For example, a museum exhibits historical artefacts and these objects give off a vibration which quietly presses upon you as you walk past. All the life journey of an artefact, from the beginning of its creation to the present moment, will be moving through your being. You may not notice this happening, but you will know how some objects are more pleasing to look at than others, not so much by their visual state, but by the feeling they bring up in you. Just as the objects are marking the ether with their past, so are you, and together with the energy in the building from thousands of people who have visited there, we have a great big whirling soup of energy.

Even so-called nice places, such as churches, ashrams and temples will have a collection of thought forms within their walls. Underneath these thoughts you will find fear at play. People may go to these places out of duty or because of their conditioning, and others run to them to get away from pain and abuse. They may find temporary solace in a place which vibrates with thoughts of God or peace, but ultimately, they will have to realise it is an illusion. No four walls on this Earth can save us, we are already living in a box and the solution is to face the walls of our own making.

What we will experience is the effect upon our being that comes from being in any building. If you are clear in your inner world and you have become acutely aware of yourself, then the space which has been cleared within your cells will suck up all the energy that resides in the building. Your cells will now be full of the whirling soup, but the good news is that because it is not your 'stuff' it is easy to dispose of. A good way to test this process is to note how you feel before walking into a building and how you feel afterwards. If afterwards you feel more negative, know you have collected energy, and if you feel lighter and happier, then some of your energy has been cleared from you.

Countries also carry with them the collected energy of the people who reside, visit or die there. Huge egregores collect in the ether surrounding the country, and the second an aeroplane you may be on enters the zone of the country, your energy field will be inter-relating with millions of thoughts and imprints of people.

Cities hold more thought-based energy than towns or villages, but one place where human thought has not taken over is in the desert, here you will experience a silence in the air, which is so still it is almost deafening. When the mind meets with this absolute vast area of silence, it can go into shock, and all that has been suppressed will begin to come out of the cells. It is possible to feel this sense of peace in the early hours of the morning when most people are still asleep, but it is a very rare phenomenon. There are very few places left on the Earth which are not filled with the constant movement of thought.

Space and time have no set boundaries as to the movement of thought, because to think is to immediately put your energy to wherever your thoughts are. People in the limelight are a good example of seeing how collective thoughts can affect people. One famous person can be dealing with millions of projected thoughts from fans and the media, and the strain of carrying so much weight can send the person over the edge. Many have had psychological breakdowns, some have turned to drink and drugs and others have committed suicide. The pressure of holding millions of projected thoughts often causes them to lose their own sense of self.

On many occasions the media have proved to be the judge and executioner for a person's rise to fame and for their demise. They help to build up the public's adoration and they can also be responsible for the negative publicity that causes the person to come crashing down. Imagine being bombarded by millions of hateful judgments? You may say the person deserved it because of their ego. They have an ego in the first place because somewhere in their early life they experienced their first point of pain, and their desire for fame may be an act born out of the desperation to be loved. There are some famous people who treat their skill as a job and they are able to detach themselves from the stage image they project. They generate very little publicity because they live ordinary lives away from their job and the press find very little gossip to fling at them. These people can handle fame much easier than those seeking the limelight.

The key to all of this is to become aware of what is happening to you in any given moment. If you find yourself dealing with people who are judging you or if you suddenly feel angry or depressed whilst with someone for no apparent reason, then you need to remove yourself from the situation. Go out of the room or the building and stay away until you have come back into your own sense of peace. If you find someone has visited you at home and brought with them a sense of unease, then open up all the doors and windows to exchange the air, as the energy can dissipate in nature.

A room is never empty if your thoughts are full, so you must always start with the purification of your own mind before you can even attempt to help another. If you find yourself projecting thoughts onto other people or places, then come back to the awareness of these thoughts as they move through your mind. Observe them without getting attached to them and they will dissipate.

The Fear of the Negativity

The mind only knows the past. Its whole movement is between the two opposite points of pleasure and pain. When you begin to look at the workings of your own egoic mind, you will realise just how judgmental it really is. This awareness of the self can also lead you into a period of hyper-sensitivity where you become more conscious of the energies around you. Situations that were comfortable to you before can suddenly feel odd or even painful, and relationships with friends and family members can become fraught or turbulent. You may feel alone as you try to grasp the meaning of this new world of sensing, which was shut down in your childhood. You have relied on an external authority for so long that it can be a shock to realise the extent of human pollution. Living a life from the intellect will numb other impulses and realities, and when the mind is laid bare, you will recognise how a huge piece of life has evaded you.

It is very easy at this point to reject others and isolate yourself, but you are not dealing with the root cause of the problem. Pushing people away through the fear of being polluted will only draw them further in, as your act of rejection may cause them to project their anger onto you, so you have just attracted the very pollution you are running from. This fear of the pollution or the distortion can create a feeling of disgust in you and you may feel like erecting barriers against other people. This trying to protect oneself from the filth of the human mind is in fact a form of pride: 'I am clean and you are dirty.' Underneath this disgust lies fear and this fear is what needs be looked at. When you see yourself as separate from another, the ego is still involved.

It is therefore important to understand the movement of thought energy and realise how every human is connected to every other human. There is much written on the subject of auras and energy fields, but how do we know if they really exist? The atom has been scientifically proven to vibrate at various frequencies, which emits an energy field around it. The space in the atom, or gravity, which holds the elements of the electron, proton and neutral apart, vibrates at a certain frequency, giving a space for the elements to occupy; esoterically, this has been described as the etheric body, it is the part of the aura which is closest to the human body. The female electron emits a higher frequency than the etheric, and this higher frequency layer, which surrounds the etheric, is named by some as the astral body. The male proton emits an even higher frequency and this next layer is referred to as the mental body, and the neutral emits a frequency higher than all and this layer is known as the spiritual body. The human body is therefore surrounded by layers of energy which are holding all the information stored within the atoms of the cells.

When you pass a person in the street both of your energy fields will pass through each other. If you are both full of conditioning, beliefs and opinions, then your energy will assess the other person's energy and decide whether to like them or not. If you have cleared vast quantities of your past conditioning by emptying the memory banks and facing your fears, then, like a magnet, you will draw from them some of their impure imprints from the cells. You cannot stop this from happening, but a lot of people with this awareness try to avoid human contact because they are afraid of these contaminated imprints from others.

It is important to face this reaction of recoil, because until we face the negativity on this planet and see it for what it is without fear, it will continue to have power over us. Yes, you may need a quiet and peaceful space at home to be with yourself, but in order to know yourself you must relate with others. It is other people who are going to show you what still needs to be worked on by helping you to see your own reactions and judgments. It is easy to blame others for your energetic pain after being with them, but is this the solution? Before you realised the need to clean up your cells and your life, you will have unconsciously filled the ether with your opinions and conditioning, so blame only keeps you in the ego and in the mind. If you energetically collect something distorted from a person, then to fear it will only keep it with you. Something that does not have anything to do with you cannot live in your energy for long unless there is something keeping it there. Fear holds and suppresses energy.

When you get to this sensitive point, hiding yourself away and rejecting others will not solve the problem of distorted energy on this planet. If the Earth is made up of the primeval atom, then she too has energetic layers which are vibrating the information held within her cells. The energy field of the human is therefore inter-reacting with her fields and we are exchanging energy on all the layers. The Earth is a pulsating life-form that has every single human thought, feeling and act running through it, so we are being affected in every moment by every other human whether we stay at home or go out to the shops. A person in India can affect a person in Ireland quicker than the speed of light without even coming face-to-face. It is that simple. This is why it takes only one person to change the world.

In the blink of an eye you are being affected by billions of life-forms. The only difference between sitting at home alone and being physically with a person, is that you will instantly feel the effect of the person's thoughts or judgments as they will be aimed directly towards you. Therefore, the feeling of being drained or attacked is more personal.

Distorted energy is happening around us all the time, so we cannot hide or run from it. All we can do is see it as a fact. Looking at it without fear will remove its power over you. For example, you go to a hotel to stay for the night. The thought of sleeping on a well-used mattress is not exactly appealing, but you do not fear the mattress, so there is no conflict and it has no power over you. If you are afraid of the mattress, then you will worry about lying on it, you will worry about any negativity lurking in the mattress and whether your back will be bad in the morning, etc. Now it has power over you.

If you wake up in the morning feeling at odds with yourself because the energy of all the people who have previously slept on the mattress has affected you, then you see this as a fact. From this awareness you can take action. A cold shower will magnetically drain your energy of what is not yours, and the act of observing your mind will highlight any judgments, etc. If you rise feeling disgusted and recoil in fear, then you will carry this with you and it will tap you on the shoulder at the next hotel. In fact you are taking your experience with you and you have stored it as a dislike in your cells.

It is similar to the story of the two monks, who, whilst out walking, meet a woman by the river and she asks them to help her across because it is too deep. There are no boats available and the older monk can just about stand with his head above the water. He signals to the woman to jump on his shoulders, but the young monk exclaims, 'No, you must not carry her because it is forbidden to touch a woman.' The older monk ignores him and carries her to the opposite bank. After leaving her with advice on how go from there, he swims back to the young monk and they continue with their walk. Several hours later the young monk remarks, 'You have broken a sacred vow by touching a woman and now you have a black mark on your being.' The older monk smiles and turns to the young monk and says, 'That's funny, because I left the woman at the bank hours ago, whilst you are the one who is still carrying her.'

You are not Separate from the World

So my next question is this: is fear different in one person from another, or is it still the same fear? If it were different would it still be fear? For example, the fear in a person in Afghanistan who is afraid of heights is the same fear as a person living in the UK who is also afraid of heights. Each person will have a different conditioning or past experience that allowed the fear to take form in their life, but it is the same energy. One may be more active with it than the other, but fundamentally they have the same emotion, so they are not separate. This makes fear a single entity which is attached to every human, and this goes for all the emotions.

A world problem is also the individual's problem and vice versa, so if individuals were to clear themselves of their inner fear, the world would also be affected. We are the world and the world is us and there is no emotional separation. If every emotion was a branch on a tree, fear would be the root of this tree because emotion is based on the egoic mind of like and dislike, and its source is fear. For example, someone says something to you and you do not agree or like what they are saying, so you react with anger. Underneath the anger is the energy of good and bad, because if you are proven wrong, you are bad and if you prove the other person is wrong, you are good. Underneath these opposites is the element of fear, which is feeding the mind with memories of pleasure or pain. Each type of emotion, positive and negative, can be traced back to the source of fear.

Emotion is therefore dualistic in nature and has positive and negative elements, such as happy and sad, violent and peaceful, worthy and worthless, etc. People often think hate is the opposite of love, but love has no duality in it. Love is the atom before it split into opposites. Hate is pain, and the opposite of pain is pleasure, which is self-seeking and therefore not related to love at all. Without fear, these split emotions can no longer exist, because if the root of the tree dies, so do the branches.

Knowing this, would it be better to deal with the root cause of fear as a whole rather than trying to snap off the branches of the many emotions? Dealing with each emotion separately can take a whole lifetime of analysing to get to a supposed solution, but is this not just the egoic mind spending huge amounts of needless time analysing the egoic mind? If you take the one which feeds all the others and deal with only that one, then you are getting to the real source of the problem. In any given moment you can become aware of your fear, feel it rise inside of you and allow it to move out without suppressing it. If you avoid the fear or get caught up in all your thoughts which are based on your past conditioning, then only when you walk away from a situation do you realise you have not expressed yourself properly. Thoughts of anger, judgment and bitterness now rise to the surface and you store the experience within your cells and organs.

When you observe fear and see it for what it is and no longer get caught up in its dramas, you are living your very own solution. This is passed through your cells into the Earth, and it affects every living creature. You have touched billions of life forms and all you did was look at yourself and see how you got trapped in the fear. The information of how you allowed the fear to rise out of your cells, feel the intensity of it, and react not from your first point of pain, but from the real inner you, is being fed into humanity. This is the genuine work of healing yourself, the human race, all of nature and the planet. You do not need to go and follow some guru in India, go to church on Sunday or pray five times a day. It is happening right now and in every moment. *You are the key.*

Is the Mind Separate from the Observed?

We often treat our negative emotions and thoughts as separate entities and we ask how we can get 'rid' of them. The egoic mind created them in its drive for seeking pleasure or avoiding pain, but now it believes these negative entities are external and happening 'to it' and so they are something which must be destroyed. But the egoic mind and all of its creations are the same thing. It is your egoic mind trying to get rid of the negative aspects of your egoic mind in order to keep only the good beliefs. Very few people ever say, 'I must get rid of being a generous, wonderful person', yet most people want to get rid of their fear or their anger.

If you were to visualise a projected image of yourself standing in front of you, and observe this image, what would your egoic mind do? It would immediately begin to judge and evaluate the projected image. If it finds hurts and pain in the projected image, then it may start to blame another part of you for allowing these hurts to happen, or someone external to you who you believe allowed them to happen. In this moment your egoic mind is seeing itself as a separate entity, but in actual fact they are the same thing.

Once you realise that what is analysing is not separate from the very thing it is looking at, then you will clearly see how the egoic mind is not separate from its creations; they are one thing. When you look at another person and you make a judgment about them, that person has only drawn out of you your beliefs, so your projection is you; it is not separate from you. For example, you are unhappy about your weight and so you automatically notice the size and shape of others. One particular person walks past you and you judge them as fat and then you start to think of all the things they could do to better themselves.

129

These judgments are revealing what you really think about yourself, or it is showing you what you fear to become like. Either way, the person is being a mirror to the conditioning and beliefs which reside in you. It has nothing to do with them. What you project onto another, you yourself are, so when the egoic mind judges what it sees, it is not separate from the very thing it is observing, so all the rationalisations, analyses and any blaming, is actually the egoic mind doing it to the egoic mind. To see yourself as you are, you have to step outside of the image, let go of the judgments as they form in your mind and come back to observing. What will reveal itself will be the truth because judgment is no longer clouding the ability to see.

There are two things watching at any given time: the ego, which is built from your past and based on duality, or there is another you, which is silent. This silence is not a mind-made silence that comes from forcing the mind to be quiet or from concentration; it is from a point of silence which is eternally expansive. It is the real you. When the mind is no longer moving over the cortex with the thoughts from your past or running into the future, there is an immense magnitude of space. Most humans live their whole life without ever touching this majestic infinity. It is always out of their reach because they are living purely from the ego, so they never go beyond judgment and comparison.

Tracing Thought Back to its Origin

In answer to the question: does thought have any power over the life of the individual?, we can clearly see that it does have immense power and it can be used as a tool for creating effects at either end of its opposing forces of good or bad. Some people ask, 'If it is an illusion, why do we have thought?', yet others do not believe life can be sustained without thought as a leading principle. Consequently, we need to ask ourself a probing question: where do thoughts come from? Only by seeing it for ourself can we begin to understand its function and its proper place in our life.

Exercise A: sit comfortably and take a repetitive judgmental thought you have about yourself, i.e. I am fat. Close you eyes and let the thought flit through your mind and then begin to trace where the thought first came from. You will find that it leads you to another thought, so keep tracing it back, thought to another thought, until you find the very root of it.

If you have traced the judgment right back to its source, you will find the creator of it is fear. You can now do this with any opinion you have and it will lead you to the same point. Once you recognise that thought *is* fear, you will need to look at the very root of this fear.

Exercise B: Once again sit comfortably and trace a thought back to fear. Once there, begin to observe the fear and ask yourself what is the root of it?

If you are observant you will find there is a question behind this fear, which will lead us nicely into Part Three.

Part Two Summary

Under the Microscope

Part Two has focused on the ever prevailing issue of: who am I? The cloud of confusion, which surrounds this issue of not knowing who we are and who we are not, is the reason that there is so much suffering on this planet.

If we are to solve this global suffering and live a life free from fear, then all of our past conditioning and beliefs will need to be dropped. This is the dissolution of the ego, as it will end the internal war between the inner male and female, which came into being because of the first point of pain we felt when presented with an act of non-love. The mind is always trying to protect us from a repeat experience of this non-love and any future suffering, so it has become autonomous, running away from pain and trying to seek only pleasure. Like attracts like, and as both pain and pleasure have their roots in fear, then we will always be drawing towards us what we actually fear.

The only way out of this mire of illusion is to go within and uproot the very fear that has our life in its grip, as behind this fear lies the fundamental reason for the whole of material existence, and it is this very thing which is what we really need to look at.

Awareness, listening, and taking action on the inner voice, is crucial for this life to count, and for you to fulfil your life purpose you will need to make a major turn around from a small daily percentage of practising this, to a huge percentage, which allows the truth within you to have full expression. This is who you are, not all the false protection and the pretentious images you wear. You are the eternal silent being who is waiting to be seen and heard, who does not know how to live from illusion. The inner voice can protect you if you let it, and it has the ability to set you free, but you have to let go of control and observe that wily egoic mind which would keep you trapped in the subtle workings of fear.

In Part Three, we are going to look at the forces that govern fear, this planet and ultimately the universe. You will have needed to grasp all of Part One and Part Two before we can move on, because what you are going to look at is the absolute unseen reality of what or who is controlling and allowing the energy of suffering to exist. This life is not a game; you are here to do a very important job, but you have forgotten it. The mind does not want to know it, because it involves its own annihilation.

Part Three

What Is It All About?

Chapter 8

Do I Really Exist?

Deep down there is a probing inner question, and all of our striving to understand the universe, God, and the meaning of life, is because of this question. You may be profoundly aware of it, dimly aware of it or it may lie deep within the unconscious. But who or what is actually asking the question? And if there were no fear, would the question still exist?

I Am at War with Myself

If there is such a thing as choice, then the real question would be: do you live by the dictates of your egoic mind, or do you follow your inner voice?

Moving through Part One and Part Two, we have realised how the majority of humans are living from their individual egoic mind and very few can live fully from the inner voice and this is what is causing chaos, pain and deep confusion. Very few people realise that the solution is inside of them, and most people look only to the external for the answer.

If total mind was created from the primeval atom, i.e. the result of opposites in action, then it formed long before the human being did. The make-up of the human body comes from nature, which is also the result of the primeval atom, so if the original splitting of the atom *is* the distortion in nature, because the male, female, and neutral separated, then the distortion existed before the human form even took shape. If this is the case, what exact function does the human have? If the physical body is nature, which has the opposite poles of the male and female residing within the atom of the cells, and we live solely from this push and pull point, then our daily life will be based on desire and the striving to become, which is a distorted way of living. If the inner voice has no relation to the opposite poles within the egoic mind, i.e. it is neutral, which is not distortion, then there must be two parts of the self residing within the human body, that which is distorted nature, and that which is not.

When a person begins to look within themself, they find these two aspects, and they realise there is a battle going on between desire and surrender. The opposite poles within the mind want to be fulfilled and sated, but the inner voice wants only to express the truth and shed the control that the mind has over the human form. It is as though there are two beings occupying the same space. Until a person begins to observe themself and look within for their part in the dramas of life, then the manufactured egoic self will remain in control. Once a person realises they have been following an illusionary self, it is easy to make a huge error by thinking you can get rid of it. You cannot get rid of the egoic mind, which has been formed by your conditioning and your beliefs, but you can understand it and spiritualise it.

The human body you occupy is material and impermanent, as is all material life. Therefore, total mind which holds all human thinking must also be transient, because it was formed from the split within the material atom, creating opposites and a movement of time between the male pushing and the female pulling forces. The inner voice is timeless, because it has no movement of 'becoming', so it is not subject to time, and therefore not governed by the mind. In actuality, you are an eternal timeless being occupying a temporary material form, but it is not your real 'home'. Some people often refer to this manufactured you as the darker twin, or the dweller on the threshold, either way there is 'you' as the personality, with all of its desires, its cravings, its striving and its competition, and then there is the real 'you' who does not have any relation to the human form whatsoever. So, if it were possible to exist both eternally, and materially impermanent at the same time, then which one is overseeing the other? Obviously, the one which is eternal must be governing things, as the material life form will eventually expire.

The Holographic Universe

The material universe came into existence from a single point bursting forth and expanding into limitless space, creating the primeval atom, which split itself and rejoined back to itself many times over in order to create molecules, which formed the natural elements that are the make-up of planet Earth. This is a similar process to the forming embryo of planet, plant, animal and human life, but the original point of creation came from the place of immateriality. Therefore material life came out of an immaterial space and it has within it infinite intelligence. This is also the case for you, as your human life was decided upon and formed by your eternal being, whom you are in contact with through the inner voice.

Physicists have also recently discovered the possibility of a black hole at the centre of large galaxies. They believe an explosion occurs before an individual galaxy is created, which throws out chemicals and debris, thus forming planets and this leaves a black hole, which turns in on itself and sucks in whatever is around it. The surrounding planets and stars resist and push away from the black hole, and this push and pull action is echoed in every atom, which creates space between individual bits of matter.

The Chinese have an understanding that when something becomes ultra female, it has contracted to such a degree that it will become solid, which is male. From here, if it expands to its fullest peak, it will become ultra male and finally explode to become female again.

The same process of expansion and contraction is what happened in the creation of the universe. When the male in the atom is so expanded he bursts forth, creating new life, but he also has to contract and become ultra female, hence the black hole at the centre of galaxies. Humans are the same: when we over-exert ourselves, we deflate and we have to stop and rest for a while. If we have become too lethargic, we can get agitated, as the drive to move forward tries to propel us on. This alternating push and pull within the atom is what stops material life from crashing inwards and being pulled back through the black holes, back into the permanence, which is vast limitless timeless space.

To understand a single atom, is to enquire into the whole dynamics of life, because it is the very thing which allows you to live as a human. This journey through Part Three is not based on scientific knowledge, but rather a whole esoteric view of why material life exists even though you are an eternal immaterial being. This esoteric view is not trying to prove anything, it is only asking you to look deeply at yourself and question your very existence and why you are living a human life. Can all the struggles and experiences you go through count for something, or do you just live, struggle and die for no reason whatsoever? Diagram 8 shows a basic creation of the material universe, but if there is any truth in a holographic existence or anything else written in this book, looking within at you will reveal the answer and the solution to material living.

Diagram 8: The Material Creation.

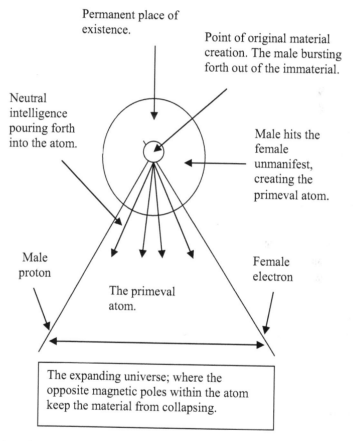

Permanent place of existence.

Point of original material creation. The male bursting forth out of the immaterial.

Neutral intelligence pouring forth into the atom.

Male hits the female unmanifest, creating the primeval atom.

Male proton

Female electron

The primeval atom.

The expanding universe; where the opposite magnetic poles within the atom keep the material from collapsing.

Physicists have recently found that when they break down the atom to its smallest point it loses its materiality and it becomes an atomic wave or pure energy in motion. Physicists have also recognised how electrons can communicate with other electrons immediately, despite distance, so an electron thirty billion miles away from another electron is able to receive information instantly. These discoveries are showing, as scientific fact, that there is inter-connectedness in the universe which moves through subatomic waves. But what does this mean for the individual person living a 'normal' human life? If you take a cup and look at it, you will feel its solidity and its weight. The molecules holding it together are tightly packed and it appears to be a material object. If you were to imagine yourself wearing a pair of magical glasses that could see the atomic waves in everything, then the cup would become a wave movement and lose its material dimension. With the same glasses look at a chair, a window, a flower, or an animal and finally, look at another human being.

You have now moved yourself out of the world of matter into subatomic matter and you are seeing forms as pure energy. This suggests that material existence is not actually solid; it is created by atomic waves, which have the original electron, proton and neutral within them. You are in fact a holographic wavelength projected out from the immaterial existence.

In 1979 neurophysiologists, Russell and Karen DeValois investigated the wavelengths of brain cells, using the Fourier theorem, (a method of analysing complex sounds or other waveforms into simpler components). The result produced the same effect as a hologram. This means that the brain is able to function in 3D, using light waves to form images. The light from the projected images also emit wavelengths back into the brain via the eyes, and these bounce off the neurological receptors, which are interpreted by the brain through memory, creating a shared 3D effect with another person. If a brain cell functions as a hologram, which is a reflection of the primeval atom, then the whole universe must also follow the same principle.

This must indicate that a laser beam of light within the space of permanence hits a mirror, which is your eternal self, who splits it and sends out one of the beams from the place of immateriality. This hits the reflective light of intelligence within the neutral in every atom, which bounces off the electron and the proton as the object, creating another beam and a projected holographic existence occurs. The human brain is also being hit with these beams, which relay information to the neutral of the atom within the cells and by using the electrons and the protons, the neurons create wave formations which produce holographic images, or individual holographic lives.

Your immaterial being is actually emitting a light, and your human self is the material effect of that light. Therefore, you only truly exist in one place, which is the eternal, and your personality and your material human self is a projection.

Diagram 9: The Holographic Universe.

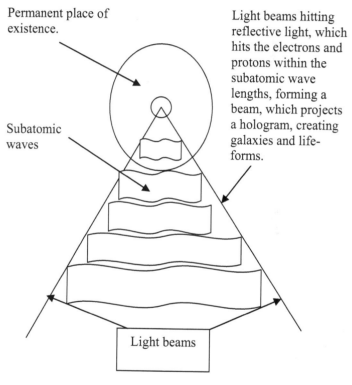

Permanent place of existence.

Light beams hitting reflective light, which hits the electrons and protons within the subatomic wave lengths, forming a beam, which projects a hologram, creating galaxies and life-forms.

Subatomic waves

Light beams

Science is actually beginning to prove how material existence is in fact an illusion, something ancient philosophers have known for thousands of years, yet it still does not answer the question of how fear was created, so we need to ask the question: as the Earth was forming, did two molecules join together and create a chemical distortion? Or is there something else going on? Why did the eruption from the immaterial occur in the first place? This is what we need to look at, because something is clearly wrong if acts of non-love can occur from a so-called loving, eternal space.

How Powerful are we Really?

If we, and everything around us, are ultimately made up from wavelengths, then the way we look at the world needs to change. If subatomic wavelengths are able to communicate instantaneously and move as one intelligence, then all matter is not separate, it is a whole movement. The primeval atom which exists in the cells of one human is the same as in another, as is the primeval atom in a flower, animal, water, etc. The only difference is the configuration of atoms in the molecules, which creates various forms.

One atomic wave affects another atomic wave, so if we pollute the atoms in the Earth, then every other atom in total existence will be affected. This is how inter-connected we really are. We can no longer live a life from a self-centred state, because everything we do has a consequence on the 'whole' of life.

If the atoms within the cells are emitting a frequency which generates an energetic force around you, then this too must break down into wavelengths, so when you think, the energy of your thought becomes a wavelength and it travels instantly to where it is directed, affecting the wavelength of the recipient. In truth, you are in actually changing atomic structure, which is communicated to every atom in existence. This is how powerful you really are.

People who can manifest items, healers who can shift illness from the body or people who appear to create miracles are all manipulating the atom. For some people this happens subconsciously whilst they pray to their deity, others seem to know how to deal with these wavelengths in order to produce the desired result. Therefore, it is possible to change the weather, dissipate clouds, and move trees all without lifting a physical finger.

Most people live life not knowing that the moment they think, or desire something, they have generated an energy which changes the atomic structure around them and their thoughts actually have real strength to cause harm or healing, giving desire a possible discernible outcome. We really are very powerful beings. If every human became aware of this power to create through using atomic wavelengths, then the majority would want to create beautiful things, but there are always those who would use the power to abuse others, and create further distortion. The awareness of how you are affecting yourself, others and ultimately the world, through the messages you send down these wavelengths, is crucial to the balance of all life.

If you were in a room full of people and you put on those imaginary glasses again and looked at the atomic wavelengths in the air, you would see the thought-waves between people. Even someone at the other side of the room who has caught your eye, will be sending over a wavelength. This is happening all the time, everywhere.

Everything material is a projection in motion. We project our thoughts, emotions, desires, goals, future, expectations and fears. These projections are wavelengths, energy in movement. They are not solid material things, but they create and affect the material. If you no longer used your spiritual energy to project out wavelengths of distorted thoughts, desires and fears, then this energy would begin to build up in the cells. Before long it would start to illuminate the cells and radiate outwards and begin to affect all that comes into contact with it. This is the true power of working with the atom in order to change energy. The ability to just 'be' your eternal self and allow the transmutation of distortion into love, without controlling it, forcing it, or striving to do it, is what it is really all about.

Chapter 9

The Forces that Govern the Material World

When you look at the pain and suffering in humanity, what reaction does it create? Do you feel pity, sympathy, nothing, pain or something else? There is something very dark, which is influencing the minds of humanity, and affecting society and religion. Is the human naturally violent, aggressive, dishonest, greedy and controlling? Or is there something else underlying this suffering and its effects?

Barry, Harry & Larry

An esoteric view of why we are as we are:

There is an ancient story which has been passed down verbally for thousands of years and it may be the truth...or it may not. You will need to read the story with an open mind and listen for any truth behind the words. The names have been changed in order to make reading easier.

In a land faraway lived a family consisting of: Grandma, Grandad, their son, Jevon, his wife and their three children, Sara being the first born, who was a happy inquisitive and inventive child. One day she decided to create a gift for her grandad, whom she adored, so she set about collecting all the items she would need. Whilst building the gift, she realised she needed an extra element, and she knew the only place where she could get it was from her grandad's shed. So, she hid in the garden, waiting for an opportune moment, before sneaking in and taking the item without his permission. She felt, as the gift was to be a surprise, he would not mind.

When she added the extra element to the gift, something seemed to go wrong, and what was supposed to be full of love and light, appeared to turn into a dull shade of grey. Never having seen anything like it before, she went into shock, and instead of showing it to her grandad, she hid it in her trouser pocket.

Throughout the day she kept re-playing what she had done over and over, and by the early afternoon, as she was reflecting upon her action of taking something from her grandad without his permission, she felt a movement in her pocket; the 'thing' was alive and moving about.

Steadily, she opened her pocket and peeked into the darkness, and as the light streamed in, it revealed a grey creature sitting on a rock, crying with loneliness, who we will call Barry. There was an energy around Barry which Sara had never seen before and as she studied it, wafts of it floated to her and made her feel uncomfortable. Suddenly, Barry realised he could see, and so he turned towards the light and saw before him a golden majestic face of pure sublime beauty. Feeling a surge of desire he immediately wanted to touch the vision and so he reached for it. Appalled at what was there, Sara abruptly shut the pocket. The creature mourned her rejection and cried out in pain, but the feeling of being uncomfortable was churning inside Sara, quickly turning into shame and guilt.

Meanwhile, Grandad sensed Sara's uneasiness, so he pulled Jevon to one side at the evening barbeque and discussed it with him. They decided to call the whole family together and ask Sara what was wrong. Sara described all that had happened and her father asked to look in her pocket. She tentatively opened the pocket, and still sitting on the rock was the grey creature. Barry immediately turned towards the light, looking for his golden love, but instead there was a different ball of light. Squinting up at its vastness, he saw a male looking back at him and he roared in anger and envy. The creature sensed the power of the great ball of light and he was livid at its intrusion. Sara slammed the pocket shut, leaving Barry in an explosive mood.

The family had never met distortion in any of their creations before, so they did not know how to deal with it. One family member suggested destroying it whilst it was still in the pocket, but this could mean Sara being affected in the process, and as they had never destroyed anything before, they did not have the tools or concept of how to do it. In the end it was Grandma who declared that the only way to deal with it was to cleanse it. There was a general agreement and discussion on how it could be cleansed whilst still in the pocket, which would help them to contain it and deal precisely with the stolen element that distorted it, leaving only the love and light of Sara's creative innocence. The only way to do this was to put vast amounts of love and light into the pocket. This would dilute the distortion and eventually it would return back into a pure state.

Meanwhile, Barry had not only exploded in anger, but he also realised how he himself was made up from some of the light which he had seen, and also a dark substance, which made

151

him look grey, so he separated all three and greedily decided to make things from himself with these three aspects. The first thing he wanted to create was a friend, so he added together shame, loneliness, pride, greed and anger, together with joy, beauty and the sublime, and thus created a multi-coloured creature, whom he named Harry.

After Harry came Larry, who was made up of desire, envy, jealousy, greed, lust, anger, creativity, intelligence and joy. In the midst of creating his friends, Barry also created a myriad of images to reflect his love for the golden one, in the form of gods, angels, and devas. After creating millions of life forms, he decided to create stars and planets for them to live upon, and one particular favourite planet of his he named 'Earth'.

Upon the Earth he decided to create creatures to entertain his friends Harry and Larry with. He took the three elements of light, grey and dark that he formed the Earth with and created oceans, landscapes, plants and animals. Eventually, Barry moulded the first human out of only the dark aspect and it produced a creature which was just as savage as some of the animals, so he fashioned another one with an equal mix of light and dark. This type was much more intelligent and entertaining.

Sitting upon his throne overlooking his universe, Barry thought he was invincible, until one day, the pocket opened and beams of light zipped across his universe causing stars to burst and suns to form and he felt a tremor move through his world. This tremor was shock, and it created a new emotion, which rose rapidly from the darkest depth of his being, wrapping itself around all of his creations, affecting everything. It was fear: the fear of being annihilated by these invading beams of light.

When Barry looked down upon the Earth, there were beings of pure light attached to these beams, and they were teaching his humans who were beginning to glow and propel upwards towards the opening of the pocket. He felt the purpose of the light beings, whose mission was to take all of his creations back into a pure state. He roared in agony and immediately placed a veil at the opening of the pocket that cut off the beams of light. He also needed the humans to forget about the teachings the light beings had imparted to them, so he created death and re-birth for all of nature on the Earth, including the human body. Those who had been cut off from the light began to lose their way, as they got pulled more and more into the Earth, transforming their light into physical matter, so that they too now followed the cycle of death and re-birth. They could no longer go home.

When everything had calmed down, Barry could hear a small cry from the humans which he had never heard before. It was a calling out for guidance and help from some sort of unidentifiable source. No matter what he gave them, they kept on crying to go home. They were no longer content with their small lives, as they wanted to be in touch with something greater than themselves. In order to put a halt to the pitiful noise, he decided to give them someone to look up to and worship, so he put Harry in charge of creating the idea of this great being called 'God' to the humans, and religion was born.

Harry took his job very seriously and created many religions, philosophies and paths for the humans to take, which ultimately led them right back to Harry. People flocked to his teachings, his hierarchies, his rules, dogmas, sacrifices and worship. Barry's idea was proving to be a success. Only a few humans saw the ploy and refused to take part.

The effect from the invasion also changed how humans lived their now mortal lives. Barry became fascinated as he watched them group together in order to share the daily workload. They were taught from the light ones how to farm, fish and survive. The fear that had seeped onto the Earth from Barry mingled with desire, so Barry put Larry in charge of these groups to see what would happen. Larry happily began to guide them with his envy, greed, power and domination, until fully fledged societies based on striving for more began to take shape. He revelled in being entertained by war and corruption, and he also showered humanity with seduction, manipulation, hidden intent and lust.

There were now three types of humans living on the Earth: those formed only with dark, those with half light and half dark, and those who came from the beams of pure light. Over lifetimes, those from the light cried out inside for something they had long forgotten; those who had both the light and the dark were pulled between their inner voice within and their desires, and those with no light at all, lived mainly animalistic lives, sating themselves through the senses.

Diagram 10: Barry, Harry & Larry.

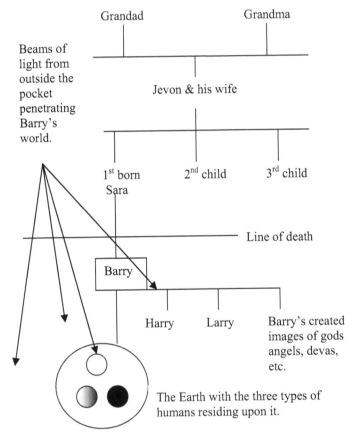

From outside of the pocket, Sara and her family watched everything unfold through Barry's veil. They were concerned, as the cleansing beams of light, who had carried forth love into the pocket, could not return through the veil and the light was quickly diminishing. Jevon decided that he would have to send a powerful beam from himself in order to break through the veil and be born on the Earth and reach those who were stranded and remind them of their mission.

Barry felt the power of the light as soon as it pierced the veil, and in response he followed its path to the Earth, and sent a dark beam from himself into the womb of a woman, so that he too could manifest on the Earth. He knew he was no match for the light in his universe, but he could affect the outcome on the Earth as a human and annihilate it, so that it did not have any lasting effect on his humans.

Once born on the Earth, Jevon began to call inwardly three times to the light in the humans. The first call was heard by those who came with the initial mission and they immediately dropped everything and went towards the call. The second call was heard by those half light and half dark humans formed by Barry, and in response, they dithered, hesitated and resisted, but eventually some answered the call. The third call was sent out for any flicker of light that may have existed in the dark humans, but the majority did not even hear the call, so they stayed in their darkness.

Jevon taught all those who would listen about their spiritual heritage and he reminded those who came from outside of the pocket about their mission. The light grew once again on the Earth. He also told them how there was now a permanent hole in the veil of death, where they could move through if they let go of all the past, their conditioning, beliefs and any attachments they had formed on the Earth.

At first, Barry watched with interest from the sidelines, but as Jevon's popularity grew, the air also became filled with tiny particles of light. Barry's world of darkness was beginning to dissolve. Outraged, Barry drew powerful men towards him and they began to plot Jevon's downfall. With weapons and threats. they managed to turn people against him, and within a short time they had the human form of Jevon killed.

The light that held the human form left the Earth and retracted into the universe, where he faced Barry. At first, Barry tried to manipulate and seduce Jevon into working with him, but Jevon only laughed at his feeble attempt to make him a king of a pocket! Barry begged for his life, and when that did not work, he became angry and threw fire at Jevon.

Eventually, Jevon expanded his beam of light and exploded it into Barry's world. It connected with the original particles of Sara's light which Barry had been created with. These particles woke up and answered the call, infusing the universe with spiritual intelligence. Fearing his death, Barry dived for cover into the darkest corner of the pocket, where the light could not yet reach it. Satisfied for now, Jevon ascended back up to the opening of the pocket, and once back home, he continued to send down new beams through the hole in the veil to be born again on the Earth.

Barry refused to emerge from his dark corner. Instead, he devised a plan that would ensure the annihilation of the light within the humans on the Earth, therefore ending any further invasion from outside the pocket. To prevent humans from going within and finding their spiritual heritage, he used fear as his tool, creating distractions, atrocities, diseases, decay, more religions, more striving, money, politics and taxes.

He also decided to make the humans accountable for their actions, and the only way they could go through the hole in the veil and not be pulled back to the Earth, was to have a clean balance sheet upon death, where all the acts of love are measured against any acts of non-love and if the balance is in the favour of non-love, the person must continue in another round of human living. Barry felt this plan was fool-proof, as it was much easier for a human not to love, than it was to love, so very few people would be able to pass through.

To counteract these restrictions, Jevon continued to send strong beams onto the Earth to form humans who could wake up quickly to the mission, see the folly and go beyond the many illusions of material life.

Barry is a transient being and will eventually be annihilated. The battle still continues today. Each human has within it the material mind of Barry and its eternal spiritual heritage, which is the inner voice. The question is: how much percentage of your day is spent in each one?

The Three Traps of Humanity

If we look at the underlying message of the story, we will find that a distortion was created, which is responsible for the projection of material life. This distortion is not only in the human mind, but also within nature. In fact, the whole cosmos is distorted, because it began when the very first atom split itself into the three elements.

There are also unseen forces at work which keep this distortion in place. To go back to its pure state of oneness, each individual will need to understand the mind, let go of religion, and create a society based on love. Until the individual realises the workings of these forces within their life, then they will remain held within these three traps of humanity. Total mind, i.e. total material existence, encompasses these three forces, and each force has its many minions that do its bidding.

When we give our egoic mind, society, and religion, our personal energy, we are feeding the huge egregores which collect from the thoughts that surround these three things. These three egregores must also be attached to their original creator who allowed them to come into being, which is total mind. So one huge egregore, or force, controls the majority of life on this planet. Barry is the representative of total mind and he is also governs the individual egoic mind, Harry is the egregore of religion, and Larry is the egregore of society. If you look around at the people in your life, you will be able to see clearly whose influence they come under. All three forces have within them the opposites of good and bad.

If you look at some esoteric books, which deal with the subjects of angels, devas and gods, you will see how most of these beings have been described as having a vice and a virtue; these are opposites in action and therefore the so-called deities were also created by the mind. If there was life beyond the mind, then it would not have any dualistic nature within it.

Those that pray to a wrathful vengeful God, an elitist God, or a God, for instance, who only saves those who have a water-made sign of a cross on their forehead, are, in actual fact, just praying to illusion. It is a human mind-based belief system and therefore dualistic in nature.

The only thing we have, which can guide us through this mire of illusion, is the inner voice, but if we are not listening to it, or we do not act upon its advice, then Barry, or the egoic mind, is actually controlling our life. We have become trapped by the illusion. Would the inner voice tell you to be vengeful, to be elitist, abuse another, murder, rape, vote for those who would create wars, let your neighbour starve, beat your wife, beat the kids, blow up an aeroplane, or work in an abattoir and slit the throat of four hundred animals a day? The list is endless, but the answer will always be the same. The inner voice does not know how to commit an act of non-love and it is your personal telephone line to your eternal being, who resides in the realm beyond the mind, where duality does not exist.

If we are here to listen to and act upon this eternal being and bring our life under the total guidance of love, then why was the material created? Why would Barry have come into existence and created a non-loving environment? Something obviously happened within the eternal realms for a movement to take place, which created a projection of separation, known as material life.

The Distortion

At the end of Part Two, when we traced a judgmental thought back to its creation, we found that it came from fear. When we asked what the very root of fear was, we would have uncovered a deeply probing question:

Do I really exist?

If you dig deep enough inside yourself you will find this is the only real question you have. You want to know if you are real, if you are more than a human being and if there is something lasting and eternal about yourself. Death is our greatest fear, because it tells us we have reached the end of our human time. If the question has gone unanswered and death comes knocking at our door, then we often panic and we try to outrun it or we desperately cling to the idea that we will exist beyond this point, because this is all we really want to know.

Can you imagine a life where you are not separate from others, where there is no egoic mind, no individuality, no fear, no hierarchy, no opinions, no judgments, no striving, no war, no anger, no jealousy and no envy? The first thought the egoic mind would throw up at this suggestion is a wall of absolute boredom. It may remark, 'Well, if there is nothing to do, what is the point in living then?' There is a belief that it is impossible to live without the mind – without fear. Is it impossible, or has the fear got something to do with not having an identity, i.e. being a nobody? This is what you will face seconds before your death, the reality of letting go of your identity, your labels and your conditioning.

We now have the very dilemma which created material life. To know if you really exist, you have to become separate from everything that surrounds you. For example, if you were to take a drop of water from the ocean, it is now a separate entity, but before you removed it, it was merged with the whole ocean. The ocean itself has no central point from where it radiates and it has no circumference, but as a separate entity, the drop has a central point and a circumference. The individual is similar to the drop: its centre is the egoic mind radiating outwards to create a force field, which is its circumference.

The very movement, which created a separate entity within the eternal, was the fundamental question: do I really exist?

From this question came the explosion and subsequently the atom, which split from a unified state into three elements, creating the opposite poles of the mind and also retaining the connection with the eternal through the inner voice. From here the egoic mind continues to move out, striving to prove its very existence by creating fear, memory, dramas, scenarios and goals. It is hugely laughable, because it is trying to avoid pain and become totally 'good' and 'God-like' in its mission, but it was already that before it even asked the question!

If you go into this very deeply and reflect upon this probing question: do I really exist? You will find there is a great chasm within you, which has no central point. When you come across this vast, timeless space, your little egoic self will panic, because it does not know how to function in this place, or what it means to be without a sense of identity. At first, these feelings of loneliness can be all-engulfing, forcing you to become aware of nothingness and being nobody; not in the sense of the mind, but in actual fact, which is truth.

Once you let go of your identity and do not react from fear any more, your life will start to move in a totally different way. In essence, your egoic mind is no longer in control. It is still there thinking away like a machine, but you do not follow it, or get caught up in it. The male and female within have let go of their battle between who gets to control the body, and subsequently the human life, rather, they are listening and acting only upon the guidance of the inner voice. In fact, life and death have become one, and your eternal self is in control and doing what its very first mission was to do, which was to bring the distortion back into its pure form.

Being a Nobody

The egoic mind always wants someone external to validate its existence. Each time you give someone a negative comment, which comes from your opinions, you are telling them, how in your eyes, because they are bringing you pain, you do not want them to exist, so you reject them. If you compliment them, then you are confirming that they bring you pleasure, and therefore you are validating their existence.

When you live from your eternal space of vastness, both negative comments and compliments coming from another's opinions are of no importance, as they have very little meaning because they are egoic based. Any movement to validate or not validate your existence from an ego's perspective is therefore not recorded in the memory banks as pleasure or pain. When the eternal being in you communicates facts to the eternal being in another, necessary action can be taken. Realisation or joy may be shared, but neither retain the moment in the egoic mind as a painful or pleasurable experience.

Going back to the example of the drop of water from the ocean, only when it is separate from the whole can it say it exists, because when it merges with the water there is no end to its form. In order to be a separate entity, it has to isolate itself by creating a magnetic pulling force, which would make it move inwards, creating a circular boundary around itself. But it still does not know it exists, so now it needs something external to look upon it and validate it separateness. As there is nothing external to do this, then it would need to create a projected form of itself.

The pulling force would now have to stop contracting inwardly, and instead, push the circular boundary upwards and outwards above the ocean and break into many smaller replicated circular drops in order to look upon itself and know it exists. Eventually, those smaller drops are going to have to fall back into the ocean and merge once again, but as they have now touched the air, the elements from the water and the air are merging, creating other forms of life, which also have the original desire in them: to know if they really exist - and so it goes on.

This is similar to the life of the human. We are spending so much of our time waiting for the validation of our existence from others, yet we do not know who we really are and from where we came. We have lost the awareness of the very power that runs through our veins, which is linked to the whole. Being a 'nobody' does not mean you are worthless. This would only be the mind's interpretation. It means being free to live beyond the boundaries of the mind, in a space where you are completely immersed in the sense of being vast and whole, where, like the ocean, there is no separation, no 'you'. This is the real freedom each individual is seeking.

There are three traps in humanity that bind the eternal being to the material world and you have to decide if you want to come under the control of any of these traps. This does not mean you rebel in anger, or you set out to change the world by force, etc. It is something you look at and see for yourself, about yourself, and you catch yourself through observing your mind, your desires and your fears. Can you see how mind, religion and society are controlling you, and ultimately, this planet?

To be a 'somebody' you have to become something other than what you are, and to do that you have to desire, strive and suffer. When you let go and allow yourself to be who you really are, you leave all that behind and it no longer matters to you. Larry is no longer controlling you, but this does not mean you sit at home with your feet up doing nothing. You are still very active, as your inner voice will guide you into what action you need to take. Once you have seen the truth about religion and you drop it, then you are no longer feeding Harry and this does not mean an escape from being a spiritual being, nor do you become an atheist. It indicates that in every moment you are aware of how your fears and your beliefs are shaping your life.

When you are observing your egoic mind and being aware of how the inner male and female are vying for your attention, then Barry no longer has control over your human form and this does not mean you cannot use your mind or you become inactive as a human, because you will be in full service by spiritualising nature. If none of these forces are in control, governing your life, then the real eternal you must be at the helm.

Chapter 10

The Haves and the Have Nots

One of the shoots that grow from the root of fear is so destructive to human life that it is actually more deadly than AIDS, HIV, and cancer, and more toxic than green house gases. It is one of the major causes of suffering, as it divides human from human and creates a state of 'them' and 'us'. It causes society to split into the 'haves' and the 'have nots' and its name is *envy*. It is the fundamental fear of not having enough, or not being good enough – the fear of being a 'nobody'.

The Line of Envy

We have looked at religion and we have seen how it supplies an illusionary safety zone for the seeking individual, as it promises some sort of salvation and release from suffering, or it makes suffering acceptable by the understanding of karma. We have also looked at society and seen how it is based on desire, which will ultimately lead the individual into corruption, through abusing or being abused, but how can we relate all of this to our daily life?

Generally, we get up, go to work, come home, socialise and then go to bed. In between all of this we also fit in the shopping, cleaning, ironing, family, partner, gardening, religion, finances, education, hobbies, T.V, internet, cars, pets, decorating, etc., but each one of these things have a common denominator running through them, which is envy.

What exactly is envy? It is comparison. Every time you judge yourself in the mirror, you are comparing yourself to either your belief of what you think is perfect, or how you looked earlier/yesterday. You may even compare yourself to others through other avenues, i.e. your car, your house, clothes, possessions, jobs, pets, children, etc. Most people are caught in this constant comparison, and we often gauge our worth against what the next person has or does not have.

This is the line of envy that runs throughout the whole system of the egoic mind, religion and society: for instance, wanting to be the leader, or some form of authority. In religion and philosophies, it can be about whom the next pope will be, or the next abbot, etc. In the new age sector, we have gurus, star-people, or those who declare they have higher energies, which can channel Archangel Michael, etc. The same hierarchy occurs in politics, companies, education, retail, etc. In fact, almost everybody wants to be at the top of the envy tree and there is a scramble to strive to become more powerful and better off than those who you perceive to have less than you.

This can be very blatant, or it can be very subtle. Sometimes we get a pay-off for helping those who appear to be less than us, as we can subconsciously feel better that there is someone else worse off than ourself. We also look towards those who appear to be successful and we use their image as the goal post or as a mentor and we strive to follow in their footsteps.

With all of this striving, are we really getting anywhere? Is it just about materialism, the wealth, the title, the land, etc., or inside do we feel just plain empty and confused, because we do not really know who we are and what we are supposed to be doing? So, in order to feel fulfilled, we use our time on the Earth to pursue meaningless things, and then we require more space to put all these meaningless things in.

Even those who live in appalling conditions, facing poverty every day, have this envy running through their world. You can go into an inner city area which reflects this state of poverty and watch as those who have nothing, try to get something. There maybe two teenagers who are neighbours, but because one teenager has managed to land himself a pair of stolen designer trainers, then he is above his neighbour, who wears hand-me-downs or cheap ones from the local market. The one with the designer trainers now has the power to sneer and put down his neighbour, yet they both live in similar circumstances. On a larger scale, they are both 'have nots', but on a scale in their world, one is still a 'have not', yet the other is now a 'have'.

The same applies to the other end of the line of envy. Even in wealthy areas, one is still a have and the other a have not. The richest man or woman in the world is at the top end of this line, especially if they have all the trimmings which go with it and the high profile. Even better if they have children who can also be exploited by the media, bringing more gossip for people to read and more envy to advertise for the next generation. At the bottom of the line, the have nots face struggle, apathy, desire, rejection and worthlessness, and at the top of the line, the haves face greed, jealousy, fear of loss, and pride. One end is striving to get out of the pit of material suffering and the other end is holding on to what they have in case they lose it all and end up in the worthless pile. This is how we judge another person's worth, by what they have and what they do not have.

Within the egoic mind we have these opposites: winners and losers. In some competitive games there are three levels of winners: first, second and third. Even then, those who come second will continue to strive to do 'better' next time. At the bottom end of the pile are the losers. In the game of football there are also division tables, and if at the end of the football season you are sitting at the bottom of the premier league, you are relegated to the top of the first division. Even though the team is now at the top of another division table, they will still feel they have to yet again strive to reach back into the premier league. Those who reside in the very bottom of the tables very rarely have big sponsors, expensive equipment, large stadiums, or huge pay-packets, so they are the have nots, who look to the premier league and dream about becoming winners.

The egoic mind would see nothing wrong with this. It would declare it entertaining, but it has created envy, competition, comparison, striving, desire, guilt, pride and jealousy. Some supporters are so extreme that they would fight, defend, and even murder for their football club. This whole process of winners and losers goes from the simple, such as playing a game of cards with your sibling, to vast political arenas, and for some inexplicable reason, we allow it to happen.

Competition, comparison, and this whole movement of envy, have no relation to joy, as this is when you do something, not for any gain or attachment, but because you love doing it. Instead, we have created this line of envy in order for the mind to keep moving from one goal to another. If it were to stop and let go of all of its entertainments and its goals, there would be this great sense of boredom, so this striving is actually leading us away from the very thing we need to look at, which is ourself.

When you are doing something, which has no relation to envy or the egoic mind, you are neither in the past, nor in the future. If the act is not taking place through these avenues, then you must be in the moment, which is love. For example, you design and make clothes for a living, and whilst designing an outfit, you are in the moment with the colours and the fabric. You are not thinking about your past failures, or trying to better any success you may have had, nor are you thinking about all the money you will make in the future, or any possible prestige from others. When you are in this moment of love, you know everything else will look after itself because there is no striving, only joy. If the egoic mind is involved, then the past and the future will be affecting your creation.

Diagram 11: The Line of Envy.

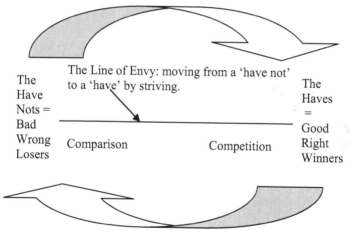

The desire-focused goal; Moving along the line of envy from a 'have not' to become a 'have'.

The Line of Envy: moving from a 'have not' to a 'have' by striving.

The Have Nots = Bad Wrong Losers

Comparison

Competition

The Haves = Good Right Winners

The fear of failure/loss, etc., keep the 'haves' striving for more in case they slip back along the line of envy into a 'have not'.

Letting go of the past and any future outcome will take the individual off the line of envy, as they are now working in a completely different space. This does not mean a person works in a haphazard way. There will still be all the usual planning and financial structure, because of the society we have created, but they are able to plan, act as needed and let go of the outcome. People who live their life this way often feel fulfilled, as the eternal being is in control and their daily needs are supported.

Sometimes, this non-attached way of being draws in material abundance and a person may choose to share it with others, but problems can occur if they are giving to those who still live on the line of envy, because parasitic and manipulative behaviours may rise to the surface and deplete the one giving, causing the giver to re-enter the line of envy to strive again in order to give. For example, there is a baker who loves to create and sell her stunning cake designs, and the line of envy is not underlying her work, as she works for the love of it and does not strive to be like anyone else or be anywhere else. She has her dreams of course, but they are not based on fear, nor are they infringing on the moment. Each day she takes the action which she feels is right and she is happy, but her children are making constant demands on her for the latest designer trends. If she were to give in to their demands, this would stretch her far beyond her current budget, so in order to appease them she decides to take on extra work. The consequence of this action causes her to spend less time with the family and money has become the main focus. Over time, the stress builds up and creativity is becoming forced. Responsibility for pleasing other people's desires is replacing the joy.

The Ultimate Boredom

As a person goes deeper inside themselves and into the awareness of fear, they will meet the egoic mind in its totality, and just before the person drops the whole of their identity and beliefs of separateness, boredom will present itself. It is the last argument of the egoic mind. How can I live this life without striving, without reacting from the turbulence of my emotions, without desire and without any security? If I give these things up, then my life will be empty and boring. In other words, there will no longer be any dramas for me to act out and I will no longer be an individual with something impressive to say or worthwhile to do. Many people believe that those who live beyond the dictates of their mind have become a non-acting being, sitting on the sofa and staring out into space, but this is not the case.

The mind's interpretation would have us believe that things such as going to the pub for lunch or dinner, shopping, dancing, singing, playing a musical instrument, cooking, etc., will all end. For this to occur, we must have a very subtle belief that doing these things is 'bad'! They are neither good nor bad - it is how they are done, which is much more important. If you are invited out for a drink at your local pub and you check with your inner voice and it says, 'Yes, but make sure you leave by ten o'clock', then you are flowing with the eternal being. If, however, ten o'clock arrives and desire overrides your feelings to leave and a fight breaks out and you get hurt, then you have lost the connection with your inner voice.

Just because you are always listening within for your inner voice, or you are being observant of your mind with its fears and desires, does not mean human life ends. On the contrary, life becomes much more vivid and alive, as each experience now has an added dimension. You are no longer being carried away with the waves of your reactions, because now you are standing outside of them, watching everything play out. You have therefore become the creator of your own life. Imagine the power of your eternal being, now imagine that power is allowed access to your human life, and just imagine what would happen if it was allowed to express itself completely through your human form. Boredom is not even in the equation of this realisation! The potential of your life has just sky-rocketed and all this without the egoic mind's interference.

The egoic mind thrives on desire. The eternal being thrives on freedom, and desire is not freedom, it is a trap to continually strive for the validation of its existence. Freedom does not create dramas filled with suffering or pleasure, nor does it intentionally create chaos or peace. Freedom is expansion without a central I, or me, or you. It is a feeling within of completion, an ending to all striving to become, and an ending to the anguish of loneliness.

The Search for the One

The greatest cry in the majority of human beings is for something indescribable, which we feel we have lost. The mind's answer to this call for fulfilment is to make us believe how another human being can fill this space within us. When your egoic mind goes beyond fear and into the vast question of existence, it peers into this place of emptiness within and it cries out for some sort of recognisable object, so that it does not feel all alone. This aloneness (all-one-ness) was the very thing it ran from when it wanted to know if it existed, so why would it want to go back into this state of nothingness?

The mind believes that if its existence were to come to an end, then it would also be the end of all life. If you are living from your eternal being, you will also recognise the eternal being in another. This being is not different, not separate and not unique, it is you. Just as when an eternal being is looking through the eyes of another human at your eternal self in you, it sees only itself. This cannot be realised mentally, or by creating a belief within the mind. It is something which is very real and beyond the grasp of intellectual thinking.

This eternal essence sees only itself. To it, this is all that is real. The material idea of separation is just that, an idea, an illusion. When that idea comes to an end, the eternal being still lives on in its vast aloneness; complete within itself. If the One we are searching for was external to ourself, then the eternal being would have to reflect this and there would be two eternal beings. This in itself would cancel out the endless and limitless space, as there would need to be a beginning point and a circumference to the two beings, so that they know each other exists.

If, as a human, you are expressing your eternal self and you meet another human, who is also giving expression to their eternal being or true self, then there would be a uniting between the two. They would become one movement, as the inner voice is the same. For example, two people are in a relationship and they are living ninety-five per cent of their daily life following their inner voices; when they need to make a decision which involves both of them, the inner voice of each will make the same decision, i.e. where to live, what car to drive, etc.

However, if the eternal being of one begins to move in a different direction, then the inner voice will become personal to that person's needs. The relationship between the eternal beings does not have any attachment to outcomes, nor does it fear, as the inner voice in each will also know the needs of the other. Just because the human appears to move away from the other human, does not end the connection between the eternal beings. There is no conflict, no anger, no bitterness, just action.

The mission of the eternal being is to bring the distortion back into balance. When it looks at another human being it is looking for the eternal essence within it, and it is seeing how active that essence is within the person's life. There is great joy when the eternal being is allowed to express itself, as true sharing, which is love, occurs. If one person is totally listening and following their inner voice, but their partner is not, there will be an imbalance in the relationship. True sharing cannot occur, because one is living from the egoic mind and its opposites, and the other is not. The only thing a person can do is to point out any illusions in the right moment. The second you try to change, guide or teach someone, you have separated yourself from them and the egoic mind is back in play. You can only watch, listen and act upon your own inner voice, which is the connection to the One.

The Spiritualisation of Nature

The real task of every human is to spiritualise nature. The second this sentence is put to the majority, the mind immediately assumes 'nature' is outside in the garden or in a field somewhere. To go to the woods, hug a tree, send it love and declare it spiritualised, is not what is meant. The mind is a material entity, as are the trees, grass, animals and the human body, making you a part of nature. To spiritualise nature is to spiritualise yourself. The mind would also interpret this as becoming something spiritual which is known, i.e. a nun, monk, abbot, shaman, priest, master, guru, etc. This is also an illusion.

To understand this very serious mission, we need to look at what exactly in you needs to be spiritualised. If there are two aspects inside the body, namely, nature, and the eternal being which is not nature, then the eternal being must be there to bring nature back into a pure state. All the things which the mind seems to think are acceptable as an integral requirement for living on this planet, are in actual fact distorted. For example, desire, fear, envy, competition, comparison, anger, pride, apathy, etc. The mind often declares how competition, desire, anger, etc., can be healthy in a balanced dose. How can acts of non-love be proclaimed as healthy if they are used in smaller doses? We are just trying to make the distortion 'nice', but it is not nice, it is the fundamental cause of all the suffering of humanity. All these things need to be spiritualised by the eternal being.

If you look at your thoughts, your desires and your fears, then your eternal being is fulfilling its mission. The awareness of why you do what you do, can create life-changing revelations. Therefore, the nature in you is being purified, i.e. educated. Barry, or the total mind, is actually learning and opening to the understanding that it is not alone, and there is something beyond itself, so it can let go of its need to protect itself with defensive or attacking mechanisms.

In each moment you are either acting from your egoic mind, with all of its opposites, fears and desires, or from your eternal being, with its facts, its stillness and its vast endless space. When you live mostly from this eternal being, the internal nature you are spiritualising begins to radiate outwards and it silently passes on the information to any material form within its radius. Even a stone on the beach will pick up on this glow. This message also seeps into the Earth and she begins the process of her own spiritualisation of nature, affecting every life-form on the planet. For example, if humans stopped killing humans and all war ended, then animals would stop killing animals and any animosity would also end. This would send a huge wave of energy across the Earth and into the cosmos, where planets, stars and suns would change their very way of existence.

The whole of material life is dependant upon every human for its transmutation, and if each individual were to be aware of their inner world, bringing the distortion into a pure state, eventually the whole of material existence would become whole again. This does not mean another explosion or contraction - it means a movement within the atom, which brings the male, female and neutral back into oneness, which is its natural state before it burst forth, split, and became material life. Over generations, this coming together within the atom would cause the material body to become lighter, nature would then follow in the same way, until eventually there would be no need for a human vehicle, and once again you would be your eternal self, and the material Universe would also become eternal.

Part Three Summary

Be Your Own Light

There are three forces which govern humanity and for ease of understanding, we have named them Barry, Harry and Larry, which is total mind, religion, and society. These can be broken down even further into being personal to the individual: *egoic mind*, or personality; *fear*, which is in relation to religion and God; and *desire*, which is based on society and envy. Each time you react through either one of these avenues, you are living inside the trap, which is within total material mind.

In Part Two we realised there is an eternal element within us, which does not live according to the rules of the material world, or Barry. It lives according to the guidance of the eternal vast space of oneness. When this is in control it is possible to live beyond the traps. This requires you to immediately follow the promptings of the inner voice, observe the mind and the emotions and do your daily work because you have a love for it, and not in order to gain or have any attachment to it.

Part Three has shown us the real battle that is going on between total material mind and the eternal being. You came into a human body to spiritualise total mind that came from the primeval atom, which brought forth material existence. You are here to purify it and take it back to its original state of love, which does not live in opposites.

This is what it is all about. When you have looked at what you are not, which is the illusion, then all that will be left is who you really are, and when you let go of all the striving to prove your worth and validate your existence, what will reveal itself is the great machine of envy, which illusion lives off whilst driving the human life.

You are an eternal being, living a human life in order to spiritualise the distorted atom and bring it back home. In the process of expressing and radiating this eternal being through the human self and spiritualising nature, you will also have a call within to create on this planet, so how do you utilise your time here and leave behind a legacy that benefits humanity?

In Part Four we will need to look at our daily life and the things we can put into action in order to bring about the need for the spiritualisation of nature and the full potential of the eternal being. This cannot be done half-heartedly, as it will need your full commitment. The eternal in you has been waiting, so do not start to open yourself to it if you are not going to go all the way. Once you become aware of all that has been written so far, it will be very hard to undo the realisations. You will need to have found the passion for the truth within you and also the passion to live with this truth, no matter what changes it will bring.

Part Four

What Is My Life Purpose?

Chapter 11

The Stopping Point

Suppose everyone in the world were to be shown clearly that both the cause of, and the solution to, the chaos in humanity lay within themselves, would they act upon this realisation, or would they continue in the old ways?

Awareness is the key. Awareness is inner action, which leads to outer action and brings about change. It is up to each individual to develop awareness. There is no book of instructions, no special technique of how to 'do' this. Awareness is not 'doing', it is pure 'being'.

Do You Really Want a Solution?

In Part One, we observed the problem of humanity as it is right now. In Part Two, we realised how each individual plays a part in the whole problem of humanity by reacting through fear, which adds to the chaos. In Part Three, we looked at why there was a problem in the first place, and we have understood that there are two parts to our being, the eternal and the material. We are now embarking on the final part of the book, which looks at the practical side of life and how you can start to work on all the areas that affect your way of being.

This will include looking at your physical state, any trapped emotions, observations of your egoic mind and the ability to create your life's potential. The exercises in this book are practical ways of looking at you and gaining self-knowledge, and if you can take action upon what you see, real change will follow. Sometimes the action *is* the realisation, other times physical action will be required, and you will be challenged to take up the reins of your life and be the driver, rather than the passenger.

It is best if you complete each chapter step by step, and try not to move to the next exercise until you have completed each one in turn, as some of the answers to the exercise questions are going to make you feel uncomfortable, and you may want to deny them, or ignore them. Sometimes, we have a tendency to jump ahead if we are faced with a question which brings fear to the forefront. The more you put into action, the more your life will flow with the inner voice.

Your Physical Reality

Just stop for a moment and take a good look at your life. Look closely at the clothes you are wearing, the house you live in, your furniture, the garden, the car you drive, the food you eat, your health and any hobbies you have. Every 'thing' is actually describing you, which includes your relationship to yourself, others, and ultimately the world. Whatever you are internally, you are externally. For example, a person who is completely focused on the goal of achieving wealth will move and think only in the direction of wealth. So his house, car, clothes, job, partner, ambitions, etc., will have only one direction. His internal desire for wealth is his external reality. This person does not have a belief of not deserving wealth, or of any failure whatsoever, so he will blinker himself to what really matters in life in order to grasp his desire.

Most people do not have this one-track ruthless tendency, as we have a split within; you may want wealth, but at the same time don't feel deserving of wealth. Therefore, each time you receive wealth, you either let it slip through your fingers, or you hold onto it as tightly as possible. There are some people who become obsessed with wealth, but do not have the necessary tools to obtain it, because they have not tackled the root cause of the issue, which is to do with self-worth.

Self-knowledge is what is important if you are to live a life free of fear, or the egoic mind, because only then can the external reflect the real you. When you observe yourself closely, you are also observing the whole of humanity, because your problems are the same as everyone else's. Your reactions may be different, but the fundamental fear is the same. As you discover the solution to this huge human problem, it does not give you the right to direct another person's life, or become an authority to anyone else. This is a silent revolution, and not a declaration to the world of how greatly spiritual you are.

It is not your image which is spiritual, but the eternal you. There are many people who have an image which is the external declaration of their religious and spiritual status; they may wear fancy garbs, shave their heads, pray in the street, collect alms, live in monasteries, wear symbols, etc. Yet others may believe spirituality is the knowledge contained in religious, esoteric, or new age books, and they cannot wait to recount their new found knowledge to people, who appear to be less educated on the subject, thereby giving themselves a superior air of, 'I know and you do not'. Very few people are sincerely willing to actually do the work silently, whilst still living a day-today 'normal' life. Those people who declare their spiritual status are often removed from the practicalities of physical life, and outwardly they may appear to have found peace, yet inwardly they can be in turmoil and confusion.

Living a spiritual life does not mean you are free from any material concerns, or that you have to live in a Spartan way. The spiritual life is the acceptance of your eternal self in a human form, a form which needs all the basics in order to function, such as suitable clothes, healthy food, a place to stay, mobility, finances, relationships, etc. All these things will become naturally available to you when you are listening and acting upon your inner voice in each moment. This will cause you to enter into a state of having spiritual abundance, which may manifest in material plenitude. If you still hold on to any lack of self-worth, and try to narrow this abundance down a funnel, allowing only a drop to form in your material life, it will be a waste, as your full potential will not be realised. It is therefore paramount to sift through all that is chaotic in your physical, emotional, mental and spiritual life, in order to create space for new energy and abundance to enter in.

The Mirror Exercise:

The first step is to know exactly what you think and feel about yourself, because all these things are being projected into your life. If it is possible, stand in front of a full-length mirror. If you do not have a full-length mirror, then use the largest mirror you can find and look at the required parts of your body as you go through the exercise.

1. Starting with your face and neck, really look at yourself, and watch for all the positive and negative judgments, for example, your face is too fat/thin, your nose is too long, your eyes are beautiful, you have a nice smile, etc. When your mind has exhausted itself, write down the judgments.

2. Now, do the same for all the parts of your body, starting with your chest area and move downwards. Write down all of your judgments.

3. When you have finished, take each judgment and follow it back to where it came from, and feel the emotion that is still trapped there. For example, I may look in the mirror and have a judgment about my body shape not being perfect. Tracing the thought back, I find this belief came from my father who told me, or indirectly showed me, how the perfect body had to be a certain way. From here, this belief has been reinforced by my siblings, peers and my partners. This has made me self-conscious and I feel unworthy, which has caused me to reject parts of my body, which is not love.

4. When you have finished looking at your own body, reflect upon your current/past partner and write down all the things you like or dislike about their body. Again, trace them back to the source of the belief. If you believe your partner has a great physique and looks fabulous, and you feel like a slob in comparison, then you will also need to look at the hidden fear. Maybe you feel you are not good enough to be with them, or you may fear they will leave you. If the reverse is true, ask yourself how you feel about them?

5. Once you have completed your judgments about your partner, turn your attention to your children's bodies and do the same process. If you do not have children, look at a sibling or a close friend. Your opinions of them are being projected in the form of thought energy, often subconsciously, and if they feel imperfect in the same areas you have an opinion about, you will be reinforcing their belief patterns.

Each time you look at yourself in the mirror, or make judgments about another's physical appearance, which are not facts, you have just sent yourself, and them, non-love. If you watch yourself closely, you will see that all of what you dislike about yourself is what you immediately look at in another, and then you judge them as either better or worse than you. If you deem them to be worse, for example, they weigh more than you, then there can be a very subtle feeling of pleasure. As we have already discovered, the mind judges everything it looks at on the basis of pleasure and pain, and if you believe yourself to be overweight and look at a thin model in a magazine, there will be a sense of pain.

Whole Health

The body is a fantastic tool for communicating what is out of balance in your life. In this next exercise you have to first become aware of inherited body size and shape, and accept it. To work against it, or to desire to be something else, will propel you back into the movement of your mind, which will make you strive for another illusion. If your genetic heritage is a large bone structure, then small and dainty will not be a fact for you. Once you have accepted your genetic heritage, look again in the mirror and answer the following questions:

1. Is your body actually overweight according to the official BMI (body mass index)?
2. Is it OK in some parts and plumper in others?
3. Is your hair dull, brittle, or lank?
4. Are your nails weak, yellow, or split?
5. Are your eyes clear, or are they cloudy and discoloured?
6. Does your skin have a yellow, pale, or blotchy pallor?
7. Do you have any other skin complaints?
8. If you are a female, is your menstrual cycle painful, irregular, etc?
9. If you are a male, do you have any prostate weaknesses?
10. Is there pain anywhere, are any of your joints stiff, or inflamed?
11. Do you have any illness, disease, or disabilities?

Write down all the facts of your health, which have nothing to do with judgments. At this point you may feel emotional, so allow it to come out. These emotions have probably been trapped in these areas of your body for years, so as you feel them, be aware of any judgmental thoughts or beliefs. If you are in pain ask yourself what the pain is trying to communicate. For example, you may have a pain in your spine, so bring all of your awareness to the pain and be with it. If the mind tries to analyse it, just let the thoughts move through you and go back to being with the pain. What is the pain trying to tell you? The spine represents strength and support, so have you been carrying all the responsibility for those around you, or have you been let down, disappointed, etc. Be honest with yourself, and write down all of what you find on each area of your body which is lacking in vitality.

Underneath the pain will be fear, so observe the area and be with the fear. For example, your stomach area may be swollen, yet the rest of your body may be in proportion. Upon observing your stomach, you see the reason for the swelling is guilt about a past situation, where maybe you felt responsible for other people and you believed you let them down. As you observe the guilt and feel any emotion attached to it, fear will also reveal itself, so be with the fear.

Balancing Your Diet

Many illnesses and diseases are caused by bacteria, which have invaded the cells. The body requires a balanced diet, which leans more toward the alkali-forming foods, and these will bring the body back into a healthy state. If we are prone to eating too much junk food, which is acid-forming and imbalanced, it is usually because we are keeping emotional energy suppressed. We do this unconsciously, as we fear the issues we have to face in order to free the energy, and this process of avoidance begins in early childhood.

Most children are rarely taught the truth about diet, so they usually swing from gorging on junk food to fastidiousness.

If either parent has a food issue, however subtle, the child will also create a food issue. Illnesses such as anorexia can occur because of issues relating to the mother, who will be either too lax in her parenting skills, or be overbearing. Control is the main issue here, as the child will manipulate food as a point of attention, which is usually extremely alkaline, and the child is challenging the mother's influence. Obesity can be related to father issues. If the father is not actively present, or if he is trying to mould the child into a certain image, it can cause the child to rebel and take comfort in extremely acid-forming foods.

The following table is a *basic* outline of acid-forming and alkali-forming foods. The information can help you to re-define your diet, which in turn will bring the body back into balance. A balanced meal will generally consist of seventy-five per cent of alkali-forming foods and twenty-five per cent of acid-forming. The acid or alkaline effect can range in intensity, for example, melon is the most alkali-forming food, whilst white sugar is extremely acid-forming. The aim is for balance, and not to become too strict or hard on yourself. A more comprehensive list of these foods can be obtained on the internet, or from your local GP or health practitioner.

Alkali-Forming Foods

VEGETABLES	FRUITS	OTHER
Alfalfa	All Berries	Apple Cider Vinegar
Asparagus	Apple	Bee Pollen
Barley Grass	Apricot	Dandelion Tea
Beets	Avocado	Fresh Fruit Juice
Broccoli	Banana	Ginseng Tea
Brussel sprouts	Cantaloupe	Green Juices
Cabbage	Cherries	Green Tea
Carrot	Currants	Herbal Tea
Cauliflower	Dates/Figs	Lecithin Granules
Celery	Grapes	Mineral Water
Chard	Grapefruit	Probiotic Cultures
Chlorella	Honeydew Melon	Veggie Juices
All Greens	Lemon	
Cucumber	Lime	SPICES/SEASONINGS
Dandelions	Nectarine	All Herbs
Dulce	Orange	Cinnamon
Edible Flowers	Peach	Curry
Eggplant/Aubergine	Pear	Ginger
Garlic	Pineapple	Miso
Kale	Tangerine	Mustard

Kohlrabi	Tropical Fruits	Sea Salt
Lettuce	Watermelon	Tamari
Mushrooms		
Mustard Greens	**PROTEIN**	
Onions	Almonds	
Parsnips	Cottage Cheese	
Peas	Chicken Breast	
Peppers	Chestnuts	
Potatoes (neutral)	Eggs	
Pumpkin	Flax Seeds	
Rutabaga/Suede	Millet	
Sea Veggies	Pumpkin Seeds	
Spirulina	Quorn ™	
Sprouts	Sprouted Seeds	
Squashes	Squash Seeds	
Tomato	Sunflower Seeds	
Watercress	Tempeh	
Wheat Grass	Tofu	
Wild Greens	Whey Powder	
	Yogurt	

Acid-Forming Foods

FATS & OILS
Avocado Oil
Canola Oil
Corn Oil
Flax Oil
Hemp Seed Oil
Lard
Olive Oil
Safflower Oil
Sesame Oil
Sunflower Oil

GRAINS
Amaranth
Barley
Buckwheat
Corn
Hemp Seed Flour
Kamut
Oats (rolled)
Quinoa
Rice (all)
Rye
Spelt
Wheat
Wheat Cakes

DAIRY
Butter
All cheese
Pasteurised Milk

NUTS
Brazil Nuts
Cashews
Peanut Butter
Peanuts
Pecans
Tahini
Walnuts

ANIMAL PROTEIN
Beef
Carp
Clams
Fish
Lamb
Lobster
Mussels
Oyster
Pork
Rabbit
Salmon
Shrimp
Scallops
Tuna
Turkey
Venison

PASTA (WHITE)
Macaroni
Noodles
Spaghetti

DRUGS & CHEMICALS
Aspartame
Chemicals
Drugs, Medicinal
Drugs, Psychedelic
Pesticides
Herbicides
White sugar

ALCOHOL
Beer
Spirits
Wine

BEANS & LEGUMES
Almond Milk
Black Beans
Chick Peas
Green Peas
Kidney Beans
Lentils
Lima Beans
Pinto Bean
Rice Milk
Red Beans
Soy Beans
Soy Milk
White Beans

189

A balanced diet is necessary for good health, but if you are suffering from any illness or disease, you may need to use natural cleansing aids as an addition to bringing the body back into a state of vitality. A skilled health practitioner can help you choose the right one for you. We put immense pressure on the organs to perform when we do not feed them the right foods and nutrients. If we have spent decades eating toxic foods, fats, preservatives, and drinking excessive alcohol, then the body will need repairing. Colon cleanses are beneficial for those who eat a lot of red meats, or for those who have recently become vegetarians, as it cleans out any undigested animal flesh, which builds up in the walls of the colon. Liver/gall bladder cleanses are good for clearing anger issues and the inability to make decisions. Flushing the kidneys can release repeated life patterns, as this is the organ where the energy of fear sits.

Finding a good healthcare practitioner, who understands the workings of the body, its organs and their corresponding emotional issues, is vital. The range of available cleanses is vast, so professional advice would help you find what you need more quickly, which will save you time and money.

Before you do anything, you will need to get honest with yourself about the state of your health and diet. If changing the way you eat appears to be daunting, start with changing your breakfast first. Do this for three weeks before changing your lunch and any snacks you eat between meals, and continue to change something every three weeks until, finally, you have changed your whole diet. You can feel the effect of any food intake within twelve hours, so your body will appreciate the care and attention you are giving it. Major cleansing of the whole body and its organs, which includes the elimination of past emotions, stagnant food and any toxic thinking, can take one year, or two years at a steadier pace. This would need to be followed with an annual cleanse of a few weeks to keep the body in a continuously balanced state.

Letting go of Habits

As you change your diet, you may find yourself becoming emotional, as you will be challenging the habits and beliefs you have around food. You may feel vulnerable as you let go of comfort foods, which you will have used as a suppressant, so you may swing between bouts of anger, to moments of grief and weepiness. The cells will be releasing all of the old patterns and conditioning, which have emotions attached to them, and this is what has caused you to become imbalanced.

Other habits will also become highlighted. For example, you change your diet and do several organ cleanses, but you still smoke twenty cigarettes a day. Each cleanse causes your cells to release a belief pattern, and you go through an emotional shift, but the space created in your cells are now been filled with nicotine. After a while, you start to become more sensitive to the impulses from your body and you gain an acute awareness of your smoking habit: the smell becomes stronger, the cravings are more heightened and you begin to question your addiction. You may even feel disgust with yourself, as each time you smoke a cigarette you vow to give it up, but find you cannot stop. There is now a battle with the addiction, as the mind is in conflict between desire and wanting to reject the habit.

A lot of people who drink alcohol every evening usually wake up feeling bad about the alcohol they consumed, so they start their day filled with the determination to stop drinking, but as their stress levels rise throughout the day and the evening comes nearer, the determination dissipates, and as they pour a glass of wine to ease the stress, they may find themselves saying, 'I will stop tomorrow.' The mind was determined to stop, yet the same mind wanted to drink, so this swing between feeling bad, to wanting to feel good, will continue until the root cause, which lies under the stress, is faced.

All habits are therefore a cover-up for suppressed emotions, whose root is fear, which is activated by your first point of pain. Habitual patterns are the result of receiving and

191

giving acts of non-love. Remove the habit and you will have to face the suppressed emotional pain. Most people prefer the habit, but the emotional pain is always there in the background. People often make the mistake of eliminating one habit, without feeling the relevant emotions, and quickly replace it with another habit, for example, you stop smoking, but now you chew gum, or you stop drinking alcohol, but now you overeat.

When you stop a habit, and do not create another habit in its place, but feel the suppressed emotions, space is created. If you go into this space you will find the very loneliness which you are running away from. Even a monk, who faces his addiction to the path of enlightenment, will have to feel his suppressed emotions and fears, until he reaches this sense of being completely alone and vulnerable. The only difference between the addiction of the monk and the alcoholic, is that socially, one appears to be good and the other bad. Both addictions serve the same purpose, to distract the person from this vast sense of loneliness.

Trading one habit for another is not the solution. The same applies to your thoughts; changing negative thinking into positive thinking, is only a movement from one opposite to another. It is a pointless action if we have not looked at the root cause of why we have negative thoughts in the first place.

When you observe something, without the influence of thought, you are giving it space to reveal its nature. So when you stop a habit, you will need to watch the space it filled, and see what emerges. Once you have felt the suppressed emotion, which created the habit, you can choose to do something more beneficial which does not form another habit.

Physical Exercise Brings New Chi

The majority of us groan at the thought of setting time aside for physical exercise, and the word 'gym' usually pops into most people's minds, followed by the word 'expense'. There is no need to go out and buy the latest spandex, join a gym, or invest in a tread mill which can take up precious space, be rarely used, or end up being a convenient clothes horse, because the best exercise for the whole body, is to go for a walk at a moderate pace in nature a few times a week. This does not mean a walk in the city centre, or the local mall, with all of its trapped energy and lack of vitality, but to make the effort to get on the bus, get into your car, or on your bicycle, and go out into nature. Once outside the city or town, the chi, or air you breathe in, fills the cells with vital energy, which is crucial to a healthy radiant body. It is natural food and it aids in spiritualising the nature in you, and if you are observing yourself, the surrounding nature will also be helped.

Before you got to the end of the above paragraph, what was your mind doing? You may have had similar thoughts to the ones below:

I can't be bothered.
I'm too busy with work, family, etc.
I'm a woman and if I walk alone, I may be raped, etc.
If I drive my car into nature, won't that pollute the air?
This is great I'll start...next week...or sometime in the future.
I can't do that, as the kids will want to come and then they will argue, demand, and I'll be more stressed at the end than when we started out!
Who will come with me?
My partner won't like me doing this, so I can't, sorry.
I've read that, so what comes next?

You have not even got to the front door, and already your mind is erecting a wall of excuse as to why you should not do something which will aid your health and well-being. Why? Look at what is really going on. What is the resistance? A healthy diet can help your body achieve its natural weight, and combined with moderate walking and breathing in vibrant chi, the muscles will tone and a healthy glow will radiate from you.

If you cannot walk far because of disabilities, or illness, then ask a family member or friend to drive you out into nature,

193

where you can spend some time inhaling cleansing vibrant chi, as this will greatly help you. If you already live in the rural countryside, but cannot get out of your home, have someone open all your windows and doors for a good ten minutes a day in order to exchange any stagnant chi for fresh chi.

Most cities have very few natural areas; the densely-packed tall buildings make for very little chi, and as we become similar to what we surround ourselves with, living there can bring us a sense of drabness and emptiness. Rural nature is cleansing, as the air is pulsating with fresh energy. Breathing in deeply this essential sustaining life-force will expel any stagnant energy in the lungs and diaphragm.

The foundation of most cities is based on monetary gain and the drive to strive for more. This distracts a person from their real purpose of spiritualising the human body, which is nature. Excuses and resistance to going out into nature, belong to the egoic mind. If you put the choice to your eternal being of a walk in nature, or a striving towards yet another label, what response do you think it will give you? If you do not go out into nature and clear your own energy and re-new it, whose energy will you be polluting and living on? We are now back to parasitic behaviour.

You are the Space You Live In

Your home says a lot about you, as the space you live in is reflecting the state of your inner world, and it is the platform from where you subconsciously send messages to yourself and to others. The most important room, which reveals a great deal about you, is your bedroom. This is generally an intimate and private place, where only close people are usually allowed access. To do this exercise you have to be willing to look at your space with a detached view, this means seeing it as it is without covering anything up, or making any excuses. Now, ask yourself the following questions:

1. Enter into your bedroom and stand with your back to the door. Slowly, look around, taking note of all the colours, furniture and personal items. Is the room cluttered? Is it decorated how you want it to be? Is it a dumping ground for other members of the family? Does it have more of your partner in it than you? Does it have more of you in it than your partner?

2. If you have any judgments about this room, write them down and trace them back to the beliefs. For example, you allow your child to sleep in your bed, which is causing you to have sleepless nights. Perhaps you do this because you have a belief that it will make you a better parent, or maybe you are afraid to sleep alone. Over time, you become frustrated with the situation, as now there is no place in your home where you can be alone with just 'you'. The sanctuary of your bedroom is being engulfed by others. There is no right or wrong here, only the understanding of how you may spend most of your day giving to others through work or family, but you need to find a space where you can give to yourself.

3. Open your wardrobe doors and drawers and take a look at all the items you have collected. Are there things you have held onto, even though you no longer use them? If so, why can you not let them go? Are these areas cluttered, or filled with old clothes, shoes, etc? Is your partner cluttering your space with their memorabilia and personal items?

4. If you were able to wave a magic wand and clear the whole room of everything, how would you re-create it? What colours, decor and furniture would you choose? In this imaginary re-vamped space, have you moved your partner out, or have you created a space for each of you? If you are alone, are you mentally creating a space with a partner in mind? Have you also subconsciously moved other members of your family out who were taking over your inner sanctuary? You may not be able to financially afford to change the decor and furniture, but you can

change all the clutter, the old clothes, and the things that are taking over your space.

Many people are going to find it insulting to have this exercise suggested to them, as they may not see this task as a spiritual act, because the only knowledge to be gained from it is self-knowledge. A lot of people are too busy trying to grasp information in order to change others, before they have even looked at themselves. You can only show someone the depth to which you yourself have gone. There is no point getting upset with your partner, or other family members, about the state of their personal space if you have not sorted out your own. How many of us instruct our teenage children to clean up their 'pigsty of a room', when our own wardrobes, drawers and cupboards are hoarding clutter?

Some people believe having clutter is a normal way of life, but they have filled all of their space with the past and they are stuck in stagnant energy. If this is happening externally, then the internal reality will be the same, as it will be in disorder and confusion. The avenue of sensing will be jammed, and the eternal being will no longer be able to communicate with the inner voice, as it cannot get through these areas of stuck energy. People who live this way have not been educated about healthy living, or they are following a traditionalist path: this is how they were brought up, and so they continue the pattern.

If you have done the exercise and taken the action to clear and re-adjust your intimate space, then it is time to reflect upon the rest of the rooms in the home. Stand in each room and ask yourself the following questions:

1. Is this space cluttered? Is it your clutter, or are other members of the household affecting the space with their clutter?

2. Is it clean and tidy? Are there any areas of neglect? Are there any cobwebs? Could it do with a fresh coat of paint?

3. If you have any plants, are they alive and thriving, or are they struggling to survive?

4. Is the space sparsely furnished without any pictures, rugs, plants, or warmth? If so, what does this say about you?

5. Are the rooms spotlessly clean and everything kept in its strict place, giving it an air of rigidity, due to the fear of being out of control?

6. Are there outdated food items in the cupboards and refrigerator?

7. Do you have any infestation of ants, rodents, flies or spiders?

8. Are the bathrooms and toilet areas clean, or are there areas where mould and staining has set in?

Every room in your home is sending out a message about the state of your mind, and a cluttered home equals a busy mind.
If you take the necessary action, but find yourself constantly tidying up other people's clutter, then you will need to communicate your new boundaries to those around you. They will need to give the newly cleared space respect, because when you physically clean up after others, it is the same as cleaning their inner energy, and you are not responsible for that, they are. If you are the one creating the clutter in your home, then why are you not taking the action needed to respect yourself and be responsible for your energy?

Make a list of all the things you have found which require some attention. Alongside these items, describe what would need to be done and the time it will take to bring your home into a state of harmony, which is harmony into yourself. Put the list where you can see it and check off the items as you complete them in the timescale you have devised.

The Environment

The environment in which you live, and the way you treat that environment, also reflects a lot about you. There are many people who live in dire circumstances because of the lack of money or education. Generations are continuously born into these conditions, and because they do not know any other way of living, they acclimatise themselves to it. Some strive to get out, whilst others turn to drugs, alcohol, or crime, in order to ease the frustration.

Whatever situation you find yourself in, you can only solve your own problems and learn your own lessons on the way to discovering the reason for your existence. This will ultimately help others, not because of any physical thing you are doing, but because you lead others by your own courage. Quite a few years ago an elderly lady booked a private consultation with me to be held at her home. When I got off the bus and walked down her street, the filth, stench and poverty was very obvious. Prostitutes hung on every corner, graffiti showing gang warfare was defacing nearly every wall, and drug dealers were openly dealing in the street, but at the end of the road was a little garden patch in front of a small house, where roses and poppies seemed to light up the darkness in the area. The house was freshly painted cream, as was the little fence, and before I could even knock on the door, the lady had swung it open, wearing a warm smile. Suddenly, she looked past me at the loiterers, and as soon as she pursed her lips at them and tutted, they disappeared around the corner.

The house was small inside, and she did not have much furniture, but cleanliness and harmony shone out of everything. During our conversation she mentioned how she had lived here for most of her life and how she knew the majority of the people in the neighbourhood, including the prostitutes, drug dealers and those caught up in gang wars. Over the years her home had become a haven for some of them. She knew she could not judge them, or try to change them, as that was down to the individual, but she never turned anyone away. Many had sought refuge in her little home, including runaways, battered women, abused children, teenage mums, thieves, and drug-addicts.

Over the years, some of those who had taken refuge with her, started to clean up their lives and become responsible for their environment. Eventually, most were able to get out of the poverty and start somewhere new. She showed me pictures of people who had faced some hard decisions and committed themselves to the hard work necessary. Not all of them made it, as some had sadly died, or given up along the way. She felt this was her reason for being here, to help those who were willing to help themselves. As we parted, this lovely lady smiled and said, 'Without a light in the darkness, how would you know you were in the dark?'

Your environment starts inside your home and extends outwards, affecting the whole neighbourhood. Take a look outside of your door, and if you have a garden, observe what is there. From what you see, ask yourself the following questions:

1. How does your garden reflect you?
2. Is it bare of plant life?
3. Is it shingled for convenience?
4. Is it planted haphazardly?
5. Is it in competition with the neighbours?
6. Is it just a place for the dog/kids?
7. Is it a place you very rarely frequent?
8. Has it been neglected?

For most working people the garden is the last item on the list to be done. Do you feel you need help with your garden, or do you feel any resentment because your partner does not help? The garden can be a major point of argument in a relationship, because it involves the use of spare time, and if both people are working full time, then spare time is a rare commodity.

From the garden, widen your observation to take in the area of where you live and ask yourself the following questions:

1. Why do you live here?
2. Are you happy here?
3. Do you feel this is what you deserve?
4. If you could live anywhere, where would it be?
5. Are you living here because of circumstance? If so, what are your circumstances trying to tell you, i.e. do you have a lack of self-worth, a superiority issue, etc?
6. Do you live here because it is expected of you by others?
7. Is it for convenience?
8. Are you sacrificing your peace to be near family, or friends?

Not only is the area where you live reflecting back to you your sense of worth, duty and financial beliefs, but also your relationship to it. For example, do you do everything you can to assist the environment by recycling your rubbish, minimising your usage of water, electricity and fuel, collecting rain water for the garden or for washing your car, etc? Everything materialistically created by the human mind, was made from the substances in nature. What you have to ask is: are you giving back, or are you just taking without much thought for the consequences?

There are many green issues, which require urgent attention, if we are to conserve fuel and minimise global pollution. Right understanding of these issues is paramount, because what can appear to be a fantastic idea, can in reality, be quite devastating to the planet and its economy. For example, there is a current suggestion from various avenues on using palm oil, or sugar cane, as bio fuel. On closer examination of this suggestion, we will need to thoroughly comprehend what the undertaking of such action really means. Land will be the first thing required in order to plant the vast amount of trees or cane needed, and some have recommended rain forest locations as being perfect for this task, but that would mean destroying acres of already life sustaining trees and wildlife. Others have proposed farmland, but for many farmers this would mean the end of growing food, as they will need to lease or sell their land to the bio fuel industry. Less food can mean higher retail prices, so now we are feeding the industry and not our neighbour. This will create more poverty, conflict and war.

What exactly is the bio fuel industry and who is going to make all the money from farming bio fuel? If we cut down the rain forests to make way for industry, certain plant life and wildlife could become extinct. Is this movement from farming for fuel in the depths of the Earth, to man-made mass farming in the topsoil of the Earth, going to solve the problem of pollution and bring a solution? The fields used to farm sugar cane are burnt after the harvest and the ashes are left in the soil as fertiliser. Surely, mass burning will pollute the air? The idea in principle is great, but the reality is something entirely different and it needs to be looked at as a whole movement, which will include the consequences.

Another major issue, which could be looked at seriously by the leading supermarkets, is packaging. Some already package their own brands using recyclable materials, but what would happen if they looked at items which are currently wrapped, but do not actually require wrapping, or they refused to sell products which are not wrapped with environmentally-friendly materials? The whole industry of farming would be hugely affected, and if they still wanted the business, they would need to change. This would seriously alter the amount of rubbish sent to landfill each year.

Hardware stores could also look at the consequences of selling DIY and professional paint products. Imagine taking back all of your empty paint tins to the shop, which then returns them to the supplier for recycling. This would mean the buck no longer ended with the consumer; the manufacturer would take responsibility. One of the reasons why this has not yet happened is because of money. Who is going to foot the bill? Obviously, it will be the consumer, as prices will rise. So we are right back to looking at this one commodity, money, which seems to be governing the world and keeps unnecessary pollution alive. Is money really the root cause of it all? One thing we can be certain about is how all industry and marketing have their roots firmly embedded in the striving for monetary profit. Therefore, does money actually 'make the world go around'?

We will not find a solution to the problem of pollution until we look deeply into our attitude to money and our desire for it, which is rooted in the mind. Having money brings us great pleasure, but to lose it, or give it up, brings us pain. If we were to take money out of the whole equation and just observe the problem, we would see the solution, and money would no longer hold us back from taking the necessary action.

Love Your Career

In today's society, money is an absolute necessity for living, so your work is what gives you your life style and position upon the line of envy. For example, a company represents the line of envy, where at the bottom there is the cleaner of the toilets and at the top there is the chairperson. Between the two there will be various positions. If you were asked what position you thought you had in this company, your reply would reflect what you believe your status to be in society. There are probably many reasons why you chose your current line of work, but does it assist humanity and the planet, or does it bring chaos to the planet? Ask yourself the following questions:

1. Are you happy doing what you are doing?
2. Are you doing it for duty?
3. Are you doing it for money?
4. As a child, what job did you want to do when you grew up?
5. Did you have any specific dreams?
6. If there were no rules, boundaries or limitations, what would be your dream career/job?
7. Why did you not choose this career?
8. What action would you need to take now in order to bring it into your life?
9. What would stop you from doing it?

10. Why would you let these things stop you?

11. What excuses are you giving to yourself that prevent you from following your dreams?

When you do something because you love doing it, what you create will have this very same love in it, but if what you are doing is detrimental to the planet and other humans, your creation will also have a distortion in it. For example, I may get pleasure from designing weapons, but they are pieces of metal built to kill humans and animals. At some level there will be a feeling of discomfort in what I am doing, but I may cover it over. If I were to sit within my inner eternal being and look at what I am doing, how would I feel?

You have to get honest about what you are doing and why you are doing it. If you are not at peace with it, then it is time to let it go and look for something which is whole, something where you can give love and receive love. A weapon built for destruction will destroy you in return, as your daily work gives back the same energy you put into it. Add this to the energetic effect it has on the world, and you will be made accountable for any non-love.

Really look at this. If you destroy life in order to create something, a part of you will feel the suffering it causes and you will lose more of the connection to your real self. For example, a butcher has to become totally separate from the animal as he butchers it. He may joke about it, or excuse himself by saying it is needed for survival, but a part of him will feel uncomfortable, as he knows deep down in his vast eternal self, that this is not an act of love.

How is he going to stop doing what he is doing when he has a family to feed and a house to pay for? Maybe, when he was a child, his dream was to build boats, but he went into butchery as this is what was expected of him, because his father and forefathers did it. If there were no rules, boundaries or limitations, he would train as boat builder. Realising this, he decides to do some research and he locates a local boatyard at the canal in the centre of the city, who will employ him as an apprentice. It will mean a cut in pay and he may lose his house, but still determined to follow the promptings of his inner voice, he puts his house up for sale and downsizes everything. His family react to the loss of their large home and they complain, but what can he do? He could continue in butchery to please them, but what would he be teaching them? That the desires of others, their security and happiness are more important than his inner freedom? Or, by listening to his inner voice, is it going to challenge all their beliefs and help them to listen and follow their own inner voice?

After three years of apprentice training he finally gets a contract to work in a boatyard, miles from the city and by the sea. He sells his small house and buys a larger house in a village not far from the beach. His family cannot believe the view from the upstairs windows and everyday is like a holiday. He goes to work and loves what he does and now his work is leading him into a hobby of intricate carpentry...

You are here to spiritualise nature by being fully present within the human form, where past and future no longer take over the moment. This happens naturally in the silence when you are just being, but whilst you are living a human life, you also have to earn an income in order to function, so doing something worthwhile with your time, which can benefit humanity, is vital. If you do something which does not bring love or harmony into the world, then the time spent doing this will be outside of your eternal being, which means you will be in your mind. Therefore, the spiritualisation of nature does not occur and you are not fulfilling the mission, so you will feel some form of suffering.

If what you are doing is destructive to life, you will need to stop it immediately. If you were to die right now and meet your eternal being, and it asked if what you did brought further suffering to humanity, and you said yes, what do you think would happen?

Your whole life, as it is right now, reflects the state of your internal life. Any external pain, imbalance, suffering, chaos, or conflict is happening because you are not listening, or acting upon, the promptings of your inner voice, which is the direct link to your eternal being. Look at it, see the conflict, realise what you have been doing, take the right action, and it will bring the necessary change.

Cold Showers: Better Health

Invisible energy is moving around us in the air all the time and we are constantly being affected by it. As you move throughout your day, meeting people, or visiting places, you will be unconsciously collecting and exchanging energy. The atoms within you are magnetic, giving you an energy field which draws positive particles to it and rejects negative particles, so by the end of the day, you will have collected energy, which has nothing to do with you. One of the quickest ways to deal with this energy is to take a cold shower, as cold water is also magnetic and it draws towards it the positively charged particles that you have collected. Putting the body under cold water can release this collected energy, which otherwise over time could become detrimental to your health.

Scientists have now proven the benefits of taking a cold shower twice a day, once in the morning to clear all the energy from sleep, and also in the evening, to clear all the energy built up from the day. The cold shower is better taken *before* you switch to a warm shower. This is because warm water is also magnetic and it pushes energy further into the cells, so it is more beneficial to clear energy with cold water first, which also brings vitality into the cells, and use warm water afterwards. You only need a ten-second blast of cold all over all the body, including the head, although you can use a shower cap if you have long hair.

A cold shower can have the following positive effects:

1. Brings blood to the capillaries, therefore increasing circulation throughout the body.
2. Cleans the circulatory system.

3. Reduces blood pressure on internal organs.

4. Provides flushing for the organs and provides a new supply of blood.

5. Strengthens the parasympathetic and sympathetic nervous systems.

6. Contracts the muscles to eliminate toxins and poisonous wastes.

7. Strengthens the mucous membranes, which helps resist hay fever, allergies, colds, coughs.

Imagine shovelling dung in a zoo all day, and by the end of the day you are completely covered from head to foot with zoo filth. Upon arriving home, you tread the filth through your house, and as you kiss your family hello, you deposit filth onto them. Sitting on your sofa, you cover it with filth, as you eat your dinner, the filth is your guest, until finally you fall into bed and sleep with the filth. If you knew a cold shower would cleanse you of the filth, would you do it? Many people cringe at the idea of having a cold shower and present many excuses not to do it:

1. It is too cold

2. I can't be bothered

3. I don't need a cold shower because I visualise myself on fire to cleanse away the energy

4. I've tried it and I don't like it

5. I'm too ill

The egoic mind is not going to want you to do something which will clear you energetically and make it easier for you to spiritualise nature. The egoic mind is going to tell you not to do it and it will throw various excuses in your way. We are not taught the benefits of a cold shower from childhood, because very few people know about it, and there is also a negative belief around it. The earlier you can teach your children the benefits, the more natural taking a cold shower will be for them. Often, children cannot wait to get in the sea, swim in a lake, or paddle in a river, yet they can detest taking a warm bath. They seem to have this instinctive knowing that cold water, which is open to the elements of chi from the sun and rain, is cleansing.

The best way to prove to yourself that cold showers aid you in clearing energy, is to take them twice a day for three weeks and then stop for a day, and you will notice the difference. It is not a psychological difference, but a feeling.

In this chapter you may have realised how you judge yourself and others, the state of your health, diet, home and environment. By taking cold showers you are actively participating with clearing unseen energy, which you have drawn towards you throughout the day. This chapter has been your stopping point for looking at your physical reality and its impact on the world. The life you are living, with all of its circumstances, is what you consciously or subconsciously believe you are worth. You have created the space you live in; no-one else is responsible. If this last sentence is true, then you are the only one who can change your situation.

Chapter 12

Do You Know What Love Is?

Is it possible to have a personal relationship with honesty and love? This is a profound question, because all people live a physical life and an inner life. What can appear as physically balanced, may have absolutely nothing to do with the balance of the inner life. What is more important to the eternal being is the state of the mind and the emotions. If these are at peace, then the person's whole life is at peace.

The Masks We Wear

We are always striving to become someone other than who we really are. If we can observe what we actually are, the striving can stop. All your energy can now be put into observing what you think, say and do. This observation of the self will reveal the two parts of you, the inner eternal being, and the egoic mind, which is your personality, or identity. This false 'egoic you' was created at your first point of pain, which was your initial experience of non-love. In order to deal with this non-love that exits in material living, you have since created many coping mechanisms: images, fear-based reactions, opinions, etc.

Another of these coping mechanisms is a type of mask that you wear in each moment. The descriptions of the masks below are there to help you look at yourself and see what it is you are doing.

The Prideful Mask
Wants to be a
winner/successful,
Attached to outcomes,
Can appear to be
emotionless,
Controls feelings,
Covers up fears, worries
and failures,
Feels worthless,
Feels superior.

The Fear Mask:
Oversensitive,
Fear of rejection,
Fear of being unloved,
Fear of taking action,
Avoidance,
Struggling to survive.

The Controlling Mask
Shouts at, and bullies
others,
Does not trust others,
Gets caught up in the
details
and ends up not taking
action,
Misses the details and fires
into action,
Defensive,
Strict control of the home
and environment,
Has a fear of failure,
Has feelings of being a
fraud.

The Suppressed Mask
Frightened to speak out,
A fear of being
controlled,
Aloof,
Independent,
Uptight and isolated,
Attacking in thoughts,
words
and actions,
Bouts of
depression/explosiveness.

The Deceitful Mask
Tells lies,
Hides any vulnerability for
fear of being used,
Always out to impress,
Says one thing and does
something else,

A deep sense of being
misunderstood,
Keeps secrets.

The Insatiable Mask
Feel that the world owes
you?
Has an emptiness that
can never be filled,
Isolation of self behind
false masks,
Nothing is ever good
enough,
Demands attention,
Possessive,
Self-centred: life is all about
you.

The purpose of looking at these types is to expose what you do more quickly. Catch yourself using these masks and observe them in action, for example, you may be a deceitful type, so the second you find yourself trying to impress someone, observe all the thoughts which want to be verbalised, and also any feelings of eagerness to be accepted by the other person as a worthy individual. As you watch these reactions you will find they lose their power and dissipate. If you choose to speak, you will now converse using something other than the personality.

To drop the mask is to become vulnerable to the world and this means you will have to get real and honest. If you dropped this charade and got honest, how would it affect your life? Maybe there is a subtle belief that the real you is not safe here, or others will reject this new you? Will being the real you bring about change, and are you frightened of that change?

211

When you first experienced non-love, you felt shock, and since that moment you have stopped yourself from naturally expressing love. Fear is now present and active, which has caused you to store many layers of suppressed emotions. The split between the male and female within the atom, which forms the basis of your likes and dislikes, will have made you move predominantly into one side of either your male or female energy. From here you are now reacting to everyone and everything around you from your box, and your judgments, which have created many images of you. These images have since collected together and formed a mask, which you present to the world. This is your lie, your conditioning, your egoic mind. This false self works from a central self-seeking space and it has a circumference, which keeps it in illusionary separation from others. This is total mind functioning in a human body.

If you can comprehend this, not with the mind, but see the truth behind the words, then you can look more closely at the suppressed emotions and their corresponding beliefs, which keep you caught in this never-ending cycle of striving to become something other than what you really are.

Your Emotional Reality

Emotion literally means 'energy in motion' and it naturally moves through the human being. If we were to stop its flow, it would create a back-log of energy, as now it has become suppressed and stagnant. This back-log has to go somewhere, so it begins to store itself in the organs, creating pockets of blocked energy, which reveal themselves through tension, aches and pains. After years of adding further layers and holding down the emotions by denying them, or avoiding them, they can often burst out with great force bringing forth catastrophic results.

We have labelled these outbursts as violence, anger, jealousy, etc., and because this energy has become so compact, it becomes explosive, so they are male in nature and affect these expelling organs of the body: the liver, gall bladder,

bladder, colon and lungs. Less compact energy can often cause us to become insular, non-responsive and lethargic. The resulting emotions are known as sadness, apathy, loneliness, etc., and they are feminine in nature and affect the organs of the kidneys, spleen, stomach and intestines.

A whole book could be written on the emotions and many people have done this in great depth, so without going too deeply into the finer details of the emotions, the following table has a basic list of the organs describing their esoteric expressive function. If the organ is stopped from expressing itself fully, then the corresponding emotion will present itself in your life. To heal it, you will need to take the relevant action in order to bring it back into balance.

You can also use the table by looking at the emotions which are currently affecting your life, as this will reveal the organ which requires help. If you choose to cleanse the organ, you will require professional assistance and information on the right cleanse for that particular organ. Underneath any suppressed emotional energy will be fear, so you will need to find the belief patterns which are causing you to suppress your natural ability to express openly and fully.

The Table of the organs and their expression:

ORGAN	EXPRESSION	EMOTION	HEALING
Liver *Issues with the father*	Sexual Relationship, intimacy, creativity, passion, assertiveness.	Anger, frustration. Low/high sex drive, stifled expression, abuse/abusing.	Balance work & play, sexual needs, sharing, openness, self-love.
Gall Bladder *Decision making*	Attitude to self, others, decisions, courage, speaking the truth.	Indecisive, Criticism, bitterness, fear of letting go, learning your life lessons, apathy.	Assertive, Saying no, balance between own needs & others.

213

Kidneys *Fear*	Being your true self, no attachments to material life & outcomes.	Fear, Disappointment, fear of loss & failure, lack of discernment, worry, anxiety, Judgments.	Love of oneself, self-worth, creative expression, Facing fear, letting go.
Bladder *Reactions*	Openness in relationships, following the flow of life, able to let go and move on.	The fear of letting go of the past. The fear of the unknown future, habits, lack of communication in relationships.	Reaching out, taking control, acting upon the inner voice, sharing.
Large Intestine *Letting go*	The ability to expel what is not beneficial to your life. Acceptance of the self & others.	Not approving of the self, intense dislike of life, stuck patterns and lack of self-care.	Self-acceptance, letting go of guilt, giving self-support and facing life issues.
Small Intestine *Self-care*	Nurturance of the self. Giving and taking in relationships & life.	Needy, insecure, unsupported, cynical, complaining, weepy.	Asking for needs to be met, seeing the truth behind desire, standing on one's own feet.
Spleen *Worth*	Female relationships, giving self time, home situation, self-care.	Rejection issues, worthlessness, no hope, apathetic, not good enough.	Self-love, life purpose, hobbies, letting go of what is not nurturing.

Stomach *Issues with the mother*	Joy to be alive, your personal power and attraction, ability to accept true praise from the self.	Weepy, powerless, submissive, fearful, lack of confidence.	Learn courage, be alive, be in the moment, honest with feelings.
Lungs *Grief*	Being on the Earth, connection to your true self, observation & awareness.	Grief, sadness, loss, being misunderstood, resistance to the truth.	Trust in love & self, surrender to the deeper part of you, letting go of illusions.
Heart *Relation-ships*	Unconditional love, all relationships, joy, life service, desire	Jealousy, doubt, loss of direction, rigidity, feeling trapped, non-expression.	Self-appreciation, love, virtue, firmness, freedom from duty.
Breasts *Giving & receiving*	Maturity, self-development, compassion, facing the world.	Over-smothering, fear of growing old, sexuality issues, losing control.	Letting those we love have freedom, acceptance of being male/female.
Ovaries Testicles *Creativity*	Sexual intimacy, affection, compassion, creativity, passion, manifesting dreams.	Low/high sex drive, stifled expression, feeling used, abusing or being abused, non-deserving.	Balance work & play, express sexual needs, sharing, openness & honesty.

Pancreas *Joy*	Viewing life as it is, optimism, enthusiasm, accepting the fact of any situation. Able to laugh at oneself.	Lack of sweetness in life, struggling, tired of life, no joy, no support, smothering, Smothered.	Delegate workload, time for the self, hobbies, letting go of bitterness.
Ears *Tolerance*	Listening to the inner self, awareness of surroundings, assimilating information, Balance.	Not wanting to hear, being led or controlled by others, inner hurt, not heard.	Act upon inner voice, not take things personally, hear truth clearly.
Eyes *Denial*	Seeing correctly, seeing the details, expression of goals, dreams & ideas.	Avoidance, rigidity, selfish, clouded perceptions, future-orientated.	Seeing the truth in life, ready for change, detachment from outcome
Brain *Discern- ment*	Memory, intuition, plans, calm nerves, logic, right action, peace,	Nervous, forgetful, poor concentration, complaining, stuck, belief that intellect is king.	A step-by-step plan, observe thoughts, let go of gossip, being calm.
Teeth Mouth *Expression*	Ability to receive nutrition, self-express, communi-cation.	Shy, cannot communicate decisions, opinionated, non-active, martyrdom.	Nurturance, firmness, creativity, making positive decisions.

Joints Flexibility	Movement through life changes, flexibility, opportunity.	Stuck views, anger, stubborn, restless mind, hesitation, out-dated views.	To get moving and grasp opportunities, forgiveness, letting go.
Nose Prudence	Breath, cleansing, exertion of self, warmth, discrimination	Probing of others, aloof, alone, lack of effort, boundaries.	Meet own needs, let go of gossip & control, self-worth.
Skin Sensitivity	Protection of self, self-worth, sensitivity, regeneration, birth.	Insensitive to others, self responsibility, easily hurt, projection of false self.	Look after self & needs, accept how one looks, love of the self & others.
Spine Strength	Support self & family, giving and receiving, life's work, freedom to move.	Unsupported, justice, fear, lack of courage, carrying others, guilt.	Letting others share the weight of life, saying no, setting boundaries, facing fear.
Feet Hands Sharing	Support, balance, giving & receiving, movement, expression.	Non-recognition, stuck, not moving forward, stress, unstable, lost.	Acceptance of self-worth, balanced emotions, free-flowing.

If you can look at your emotions, without judging or trying to change anything, something will happen. Observation is love, so as you see the patterns in yourself, the energy which was stuck will start to move and you may feel emotional. Once this energy is felt and released, the organ will regain some of its energetic balance and movement. Physical illness occurs because of blocked energy in the body.

Do You Value Yourself?

The human psyche has a deep-rooted belief of not being worthy of love, but where does this come from? Society and religion have systems where you are rewarded for good behaviour and punished for bad behaviour, so you are taught from childhood how to strive for the rewards and stay clear of any punishment. Good behaviour brings pleasure to those around you, so you are given affection in return and a sense of worth follows, but bad behaviour brings pain, so you are rejected, and a lack of worth creeps in. This drive to have someone or something external validate your worth is the cause of so much suffering. From the very first moment you were shown non-love, you have been striving to be loved, but this is from a point of fear, and everyone is doing it. Some find validation in wealth, others in social standing, status and superiority. But underneath all of this, you are frightened of not being deemed as lovable. All because you do not know who you really are.

In order for the egoic mind to obtain validation of its worth it will have to compare you with someone else, so competition, pleasure and pain have now taken root in your life. You may join a group of like-minded people in order to get a sense of what is acceptable and therefore worthy. These groups are your measuring stick of how socially valuable you are in the eyes of society. You may even reach the top of these groups and become a chairperson, or a well-respected organiser, but has the inner sense of being lost ended, or are you just fooling yourself with this idea of external worth?

The egoic mind has two levels of worth: worthless, and superior, and depending on the circumstance, we act out one of these levels of worth. Say, as a child, you were given very little encouragement and guidance from your parents on how to live creatively, so most of your little gifts of picked flowers, your paintings, and your ability to make shapes out of the clouds, went unnoticed, or ignored. This brought about a feeling of being overlooked, or unheard, and you reacted by emotionally rejecting them. Now, as an adult, you can create amazing things, but you brush them off as nothing, and you never actually take a moment to feel the wonder of what you are able to produce. The feeling of not receiving credit where it is due is continuing, but you are the one now doing it to yourself. By continuing the childhood patterns, you are striving to prove yourself lovable, yet you are rejecting love at the same time, and you are in confusion.

Does the external praise or rejection of what you do really matter if it only validates the egoic mind's sense of worth? Therefore, is there such a thing as real worth, which does not come from the opposites within the mind? Can the eternal being, which is who you really are, feel its own worth? It must be in touch with something, because it knows who or what it is, and if there is a deep knowing of this endless vast, limitless space, then this must be its worth. This is the real power, as it knows it is everything, and nothing can overcome it, so it is itself without any fear. Only fear stops this power within you from flowing and moving.

To feel this vast sense of worth, or power, you must first accept it. The rejection of it, or any attempt to use it for personal gain, is to lose it. This acceptance of who you truly are is the realisation of the absolute power within you, which is love. To accept your worth, is to love yourself. Not in the egoic mind's sense, which would have you declare to the world how great and powerful you are, but it comes quietly from within and you feel a great expansiveness and all the conflict ends. You cannot do this with your mind by thinking acceptance, as this is just the personality trying to imagine its worth. When you let go of striving for worth, and let go of your self-pity at feeling worthless, only then can you open the window to this majestic world. You cannot go to it, as this would be a movement within the mind. It comes to you when the mind is still, and when fear is no longer present.

The egoic mind would tell you to seek your worth through intellectual knowledge, and there are many external authorities, institutions or philosophies available to give the mind what it is seeking. Most of these will have devised systems based on hierarchy, but if you enter into these mind-based systems and find yourself lacking, you will nose-dive in the view of your supposed worth and the journey of striving will begin. You are already eternal, vast and limitless, so to put yourself into a funnel according to some intellectual idea, is absolutely ridiculous. There is no state of being lower than, or greater than, when you are living beyond the mind, because it is the mind which has created the opposites of good and bad, and separation.

The exalted good within the mind, is the farthest positive point, which holds all the highest thoughts of human thinking, so deities, archangels, higher beings, celestial guides, etc., will exist there, but they are still just the creations of the mind. If there are beings which exist beyond the mind, would they be separate from 'you', if the 'one' is all that exists? Therefore, any deity or celestial guide, which separates one from another, was created by the mind, which makes them transient and not eternal at all. Yes, they may be able to see the universe and all that is within it, because it is mind, but they cannot see into the energy which lives beyond mind. Those who say they are channelling supposed archangels, etc., are only channelling the mind. It may sound amazing with lots of words, descriptions, levels, paths, authority, raising the consciousness, etc., but none will show you the 'real you', because they come from separation. It is the inner life which really matters, as it is this which affects the whole cosmos. When you go within, you enter into an endless journey and what you see there will be real, and you will 'know' this because all 'striving' and 'becoming' will have ended.

Know yourself first and *then* you will communicate with that which lives in truth and beyond the mind. It is not the other way around. You cannot search with the mind to discover truth, as all you will find is more of mind, which will lead to further confusion and suffering. Everything you do can lead to self-knowledge, so to put on clean clothes, eat a balanced diet, live in a harmonious home, observe your mind and emotions, express yourself honestly and face your fears, is living your own self-worth, from the tiniest atom within, to radiating it out into the world.

Your Intimate Relationship

If you have looked at your first point of pain and seen how you have continued the patterns of fear throughout your life, then you should be able to see the inner dynamics of your personal intimate relationship. From your previous list of all the qualities which your ideal male and female would have, you should now be clear about how you need to be these things yourself before you can attract it from another.

Like will always attract like, i.e. what is going on internally, will attract the same externally, so your external relationship is the other half of your energy in action. For example, if you are living a suppressed life with an air of victimisation, you will attract towards you a person who will bully you and confirm your victimised state. The same if you are arrogant and superior, you will attract to yourself a person who is frightened to speak out and be assertive, because this is what is going on inside of you. Your male is in control and your female is weak and helpless.

Exercise: Ask yourself the following key questions about your current or past relationship:

1. Why did you choose your current partner? Was it their looks, personality, status, sexual chemistry, etc?
2. Over time have you grown closer or further apart? What is doing this?
3. Is there anything you begrudge in your partner?
4. Do you think/believe your partner begrudges anything about you?

5. Do you tolerate anything in your relationship? If yes, does this bring you pain, or cause you to suppress your emotions?

6. Do you argue? If so, is it about major issues, or do you accumulate the petty things until they become major issues?

7. Does your partner constantly complain, criticise, or ignore you? Do you do this to your partner?

8. Do think your partner is a mind reader and get upset when certain things are not done, or carried out?

9. Describe your sexual relationship: is it loving, uncomfortable, duty-bound, fun, or abusive?

10. Do you spend any time together doing recreational hobbies and having fun? If not, why not? Is there a communication problem?

Looking at the answers to these questions, what is your partner teaching you about yourself? Whatever it is, see it as a fact and do not try to hide it, or cover it up. You have created these patterns because of your beliefs, conditioning and fears. Maybe your relationship is a reflection of your parents' relationship, so you are just playing a repetitive role? Or are you creating relationships which are totally opposite to that of your parents in order to gain security, or break out of rigidity?

Your partner is the closest human to you who can show you all that you are doing unconsciously. It does not matter whether your relationship is formed through heterosexual or gay tendencies, the same principles apply to all. You have within you an inner male and an inner female and your partner will be reflecting the opposite of you. For example, if you are a man who has predominantly female reactions, then your partner will most likely be predominantly male in their reactions.

Love is love, whether it is between heterosexual or gay partners. There is so much guilt and shame around same-sex relationships, which creates stigma and fear. People turn to their own gender usually for one or more of the following reasons:

1. They received abuse from someone of the opposite gender when they were children, so they reject that gender and look to someone of the same sex.

2. They were caught at an impressionable age and have since chosen to continue in same-sex relationships.

3. They were forced into same-sex relations when circumstances led them into prostitution and control by pimps.

4. They have very strong aggressive energy, so they are looking for the feminine quality in females and males in order to be the power within the relationship. Conversely, both men and women who have a pronounced feminine energy are looking for a dominant male energy to protect them.

5. They were born with an innate attraction to those of the same sex.

Many people believe that gays can be made 'normal'. But who or what declared that heterosexuality is right and same-sex relationships are wrong? It could only be a creation from the human mind, since 'right' and 'wrong' are involved. If those people from points 1 to 4 were not naturally born this way, but were turned by society, then this would be heterosexual people becoming gay, and some institutions seem to believe it is possible to turn someone back into being a 'good' human being once again. Is that all there is to it, just press a psychological switch, or is there something else going on?

Society finds point number 5 the most problematic: people who are naturally born attracted to those of the same sex. If you can 'heal' those turned by society, what can the 'solution' be for people born to love those of the same gender? We need to get to the truth of this issue, which divides humans, in order to end all the judgments and the rejection.

Imagine you have died, and your personality meets with your eternal being in a beautiful garden. Before your personality can walk into the eternal being and merge as one, there are some questions, which need to be answered by your personality.

Eternal being: Did you hear me talking to you?

Personality: Yes, I listened for you in every moment.

Eternal being: Did you put what I said into action?

Personality: Yes, most of the time I did and when I did not, I knew it was fear holding me back.

Eternal being: Did you help all those that were sent to you?

Personality: Yes, I gave my all in every way you told me to.

Eternal being: Did you love?

Personality: Yes, I loved greatly and found the one you told me about.

Eternal being: Did you share the journey with them?

Personality: Yes, but we suffered a great deal from the judgments of others.

Eternal being: But did you love them anyway?

Personality: Yes, I did not walk away from love even though I was persecuted for it, because I loved someone from the same sex as myself.

Eternal being: Would you return to Earth and love this way again if it were asked of you?

Personality: Yes, I would I do anything love asks of me.

Eternal being: Then you have truly loved and been blessed with love in return.

Personality: What of those who were ignorant and judgmental?

Eternal being: They are blind with their own conditioning and they have yet to understand that love only loves itself and knows only itself, regardless of transient human gender.

Personality: So, to love someone of the same sex is not wrong?

Eternal being: If you look at a flower and see love, you have seen me, if you look at a child, and see love, you have seen me, if you look at your partner and see love, you have seen me, and I am all of life, so how can love be wrong? Only a mind would say it has to be 'this way' or 'that way'. Separation, judgment and opinion is not love.

The truth is - you are here to love and be loved. This 'whole' way of being spiritualises nature and brings it back into eternal harmony. Your intimate relationships are revealing all that is not love within you. If you can drop your conditioning, your labels, identity, striving, anger, jealousy, etc., and be fully yourself with another human being, regardless of gender, then you are truly sharing the journey of life.

What is Love?

Within a twenty-four hour day, what percentage of your relationship is love? For example, you may spend twenty per cent of the time disagreeing, thirty per cent on non-listening, twenty per cent on the games of intent and manipulation, and twenty per cent on fulfilling your desires, so this means only 10% of your relationship is actually love.

Broken down into hours, you spend two hours and forty minutes out of a twenty-four hour period, being in love. This is when total listening, communication, affection without intent, no judgments, or opinions are taking place. This can be whilst you are physically with them, or by thinking about them. You are therefore tolerating twenty-one hours and twenty minutes in a state of non-love, which is ninety per cent of your day...your year...your life.

If you cannot solve this issue of non-love within your intimate relationship, then you can hardly solve it with the rest of the world. Your partner is 'you' in the closest proximity available, and you are accepting ninety per cent of non-love in your relationship, just so you can receive that little bit of love. But as this person is reflecting the other half of the inner you, how much you actually love yourself is being revealed, which is just ten per cent.

Within the ninety per cent of non-love there will be many things which stop unity from occurring. If you look closely at all these things, you will see how they stem from beliefs, which is the mind. Most people are therefore having a mind-based intimate relationship, which has nothing to do with love. Is it possible to turn that around? To do so would mean letting go of your beliefs, your opinions and your expectations. It would also require you to look closely at what you believe love to really be. Ask yourself if love is any of these:

1. When another does all the housework, cooking, cleaning and shopping without any input from you?
2. When you are obedient to the whims of your partner?
3. When they do what you tell them to?
4. Being quiet, holding back your feelings and ignoring others?
5. Constantly demanding attention?
6. Talking and never listening?
7. Allowing your partner to make all the decisions in case you make a mistake?
8. Constantly trying to change your partner into the way you believe they should be?
9. Treating them like a child or a parent?
10. Making promises you know that you can't carry out, in order to keep them happy?
11. Doing things through duty, because you believe that is what is expected of you?
12. Making work, other people and desires more important than the needs of your partner?
13. Physically, sexually, emotionally, or mentally abusing them?
14. Receiving abuse?

Love is not what you do; it is when you stop doing. In other words, the mind is always striving, moving, changing things and becoming, but love is constant. It is not doing any of these things, so when you stop living from the mind, you start loving.

Exercise: Letting go.

Imagine being on an island, where the sun is shining and the gentle breeze keeps you cool. Looking over the azure ocean all is calm and peaceful. As you sit on the soft sand, can you imagine yourself without any past? Every time a thought comes into your mind, you let it go, because it is a memory from the past and it has no meaning here. If you have any thoughts of the future, can you do the same and let them dissipate, as there is nowhere to go, nothing to achieve, only this moment. On the horizon you see a figure far away and as they get near, you realise it is your partner. Looking at them, can you let go of your judgments, opinions, past history, expectations and future dreams? What do you see?

If you have dropped everything, all that remains will be love. This is how it is possible to have a relationship with honesty, because honesty is love and vice versa. If you have looked at the suppressed emotions and allowed them to surface, your energy will once again flow naturally, but if you do not express yourself honestly in every moment, you will once again suppress this flow within you. Honesty is never a done, it is always a constant action.

Chapter 13

Observe Your Mind and Be Free

We spend so much time seeking knowledge about things which have very little meaning. We label everything we see and we want to know about the Universe, God, or the latest celebrity gossip, but do we really want to find out about ourself, not the illusionary self, but the 'real' self? Have you ever watched your mind and the thoughts you have? Not by using any system such as meditation, etc., but just watching as you go about in your daily life?

Your mind is the illusionary 'you'.

Contradictory Living

We are in conflict within, between how things are and how we want them to be. For example, you may be angry, and you believe the way out of the anger is to strive for peace, which is its opposite. On the way to obtaining peace, you still remain angry and you still react, and express this anger. Therefore, you never actually arrive at a state of total peace. How can you when the journey has been partnered with anger?

Is there any way to solve this issue of contradiction within us? Not by moving into an opposite, or setting up future goals, or by striving to achieve, but is there a way to look within and deal with this conflict, in this moment, not next week, or in a few months' time when you have reached a supposed point, but right now?

The first thing to ask yourself is: what exactly are you striving for? Is it for freedom, peace, money, or security, etc? Are you striving to give those around you a better life than you had, and if they do not do what you advise, does it bring up a sense of frustration in you, which is still anger?

Once you know what it is you are striving for, look at its opposite, because that is exactly what is going on right now in your life. For example, maybe you grew up in poverty, where you had very little and life was a struggle. Now, as a parent, you want to give your children everything they ask for. You do this because you believe this is an expression of your love, but in fact, you are striving to fulfil their desires, so that they do not feel the pain of suffering. Therefore, can you look at what you are doing without accepting it or denying it, just see it as it is and admit it to yourself: 'I am afraid my children will not feel loved unless they have everything, because that is how I felt, and deep down, how I still feel. I am angry at the struggle I had to face,' and so on.

Ultimately, the root will be fear, but the emotions which have become trapped are the emotions of anger. Both consciously and subconsciously, we are all upset with the acts of non-love on this planet, and if people do not do, or say things, which you believe are love, you will become angry. Your definition of love is the opposite of what is really going on, but your definition is an illusion.

The world is not at peace, because we are not at peace. We are striving for peace, but we cannot reach this ideal, or goal, because we are in fact angry. We are angry at the world, at each other and at ourselves. We are angry because we are giving and receiving acts of non-love ninety per cent of the time.

When you actually realise what you are doing, there is a moment of stillness, and your mind stops. This realisation is self-knowledge, as you have learnt something about yourself which is not based on the opinions of the personality, but factual understanding. The action from this point cannot be forced, trained, or instigated, because the realisation will be doing the work.

For example, you are sitting in a room with no doors or windows and with you in the room is a snake. Immediately, your mind is alert and attentive. You are not forcing or controlling the mind into this state of acute momentary living, it is happening by itself. You are aware of every movement of the snake and where exactly it is in the room. In this moment you are not thinking about your past, nor are you focused on the future, you are fully present in the room with the snake. This is realisation in action.

Realisation means becoming acutely aware of this deep-rooted underlying anger and your expectations of yourself and others. The second you are about to enter into the old patterns, the realisation will warn you and you take the necessary action. If you judge yourself after the warning, then you are back in the mind again.

The Energetic Pockets of the Mind

There is an exercise called the 11X22's, which is described in detail in my previous book, The True Dynamics of Relationships. This exercise has the ability to sift the mind of its judgments and patterns. You write a sentence, which is a positive statement and your mind reacts by throwing out all it believes about the sentence, and why that positive thing is not happening in your life. For example, I may write, 'I am healthy and happy', but my mind would churn out all the reasons why I am not healthy and happy. If I write these reasons under the sentence, until my mind slows down, and then repeat the sentence again and again, the mind will react with yet another set of reasons. This sentence needs to be written twenty-two times, in one sitting, for eleven consecutive days.

This is not a mantra, or a positive affirming exercise, it is process of finding out the root cause of why you are not healthy and happy in your life. It is revealing all the thoughts which often run unconsciously across the cortex of the brain. You can see this in action when someone pays you a compliment. They may say, 'You are looking really well'. Immediately, your mind reacts and you either reject the compliment, by stating all the reasons why you do not actually feel great, or you accept it, and tell them all the reasons why you feel great is due to something or somebody else.

If life is treating you well, you may feel great. If life is hard, or you are ill, or find yourself struggling, then you may not feel very healthy and happy.

Each time a person speaks to you their words will be bringing forth a reaction from your mind. This reaction is your beliefs, your past and your conditioning. The 11X22's exercise is to be used as a tool in aiding the emptying of the memory banks. If you are aware and observant of yourself, listening to the words of another can also do the same thing.

Observation of the Mind

You may say observing yourself is just too hard and not really for you, so what else is your life about? Is it just about acquiring the next promotion, the next fix, house, car, relationship, etc? Can life be that fickle, where all you do is strive for future goals, get angry when you cannot obtain your desires, age before you reach your destination, and maybe die unfulfilled? Perhaps you have already obtained all the wealth and position a person would ever need in one lifetime, but still this sense of distrust and loneliness is ever present?

The mind is always moving from how 'it is' to how it 'should be'. This is its nature. If you live in the mind, then you too will follow this course. Once you see the folly of striving to become something other than what you are, you will drop the mind, just as you would drop a hot piece of coal.

This does not mean thought will become obsolete, that would be a childish view, but it does mean thought is only functioning in a factual way, for example, if I cross the road in front of an oncoming truck and it hits me, I will die, but if I am approaching a road and the visual impact of the road travels through my eyes and triggers a memory of how to function at the roadside, I will therefore take a moment to look. What has gone from you is all the psychological babble, which fear thrives on, and your mind is now working from the practical points of living a human life. If there is no past infringing on the moment, and no striving for the future affecting your peace, then you are living beyond the mind.

Fear is no longer the central point of your life, as the egoic mind has therefore dissolved and you are free from total mind or 'Barry'. This means your eternal being has control of your human life. The eternal being is love, but you cannot search for it, or demand that it makes itself present, or try to possess it. It only comes into being when all that is not love is no longer governing your life.

Can you say exactly what love is? You may say joy, peace, harmony, etc., and you may strive for some future goal in order to obtain it, but if you look at yourself and see, for a fact, all the non-love in you, then you can observe this non-love and become intimately acquainted with it. This is self-knowledge. When you see how non-love, or fear, is demanding attention from you, but you no longer feed it because you have seen and understood its game, what will happen to it? It will perish, and what you seek is what will be left behind. The mind moves from one point to another and when you stop and observe this movement, a stillness occurs and you are no longer travelling within the world of opposites, instead, you are emerging as one with love, which is infinite movement, because it has no opposite and no end.

Who are You Going to Pray to?

Is it possible to discover the ineffable, sublime and unknowable, and be in communication with it without having an image of it? Most people, when they are meditating, sitting in a church or temple, or asking for help in a dire situation, pray to a deity, which has some sort of form or image. It is very important to be clear with yourself exactly to whom, or what, you are giving your energy in prayer. Within the mind there is both the exalted good or the highest point of positivity and the darkest regions of squalor or the furthest point of the negativity, so you have to become aware of how thought travels to its creator, which is total mind. The exalted mind-created deities receive your thought energy and they may answer back, but, by the time the answer has penetrated through the trillions of thoughts within the ether to reach you, there is very little of the exalted mind left in it.

Is it worth it then to pray, if all you are doing is praying to the good part of total mind? Doesn't that put you at the mercy of this total mind? Just think of all those times you have recited words, or you have sat for hours repeating a mantra, or prayed over beads, a statue, or a cross? Whatever it is you have been doing, if you have used language and just bounced the words off your mind, without a deep resonant feeling, then you have only prayed into total mind.

So, is there such a thing as real prayer, which reaches beyond the mind and is heard and answered by something, which has not been made, or invented, by the human mind? If that is so, then this 'something' does not have wings, robes, or a long beard, nor is it a goddess or a god, and neither is it a mental concept of the Universe. Maybe this elusive 'thing', which we are all searching for, is personal to each individual, and maybe only the heart has a true inkling of its connection to it, its divine essence. Hierarchy, paths, systems, isms, rituals, worship and dogma have no relevance here. You would need to communicate with feeling to get to this place, although words which do not carry fear can be there.

Throughout this book, have you discovered and realised for yourself the two 'things' which exist within you, your eternal being and your impermanent nature being, which is not eternal? If so, you now have the basis for real prayer. Thought is language, words, and belongs to the mind, but there are no words to describe this divine essence, because it is unknowable and the mind works only in the region of the known. Feeling is not taught and it has been with you always, so feeling is in communication with it. Therefore is it possible to feel prayer rather than just think it? Is it possible to pray to your eternal being, which is this divine essence, without the mind producing an image, a label, desire, or any attachment to an outcome?

Words carry the energy of pleasure and pain, simply because humans have ploughed millions of thoughts of like or dislike into one word. For example, when you sit quietly and think of the word 'Allah' it has a certain feel about it, as does the word 'prison'. Therefore, words have the ability to affect our state of mind, hence the use of mantras, to bring about a certain state of mind. But if you get attached to the word and just reel it off habitually, then you have not prayed completely, because the heart-based feeling is missing, and the words are just empty and meaningless.

It is fine to use a certain group of words in order to direct yourself within, but once in the heart, you will need to be able to let go of the words and enter fully into the vast space and just feel. This makes the deity not something outside of you, up in the sky somewhere, but inside of you, closer than hands and feet. This is intimate communication with the real you, who is the eternal divine essence. This can only be experienced and not explained with mere words.

You will no longer want to go somewhere to pray, or make time to pray, or pray when you are in dire need; because you will be too busy praying! Living from this space within your self is prayer in action. The only way to move out of it is when the egoic mind lures you away.

Are Issues from the Past Affecting the Moment?

If you were to look across your life at your relationships with key people: parents, siblings, partners, children, friends, work colleagues, etc., are there any unfinished issues? Have you said everything you needed to say? Have you expressed yourself fully and honestly? You know when there are issues to be dealt with, because the mind is always re-playing scenarios of the past in order to come to some sort of conclusion.

If you find this occurring, you need to take action to bring these issues to an end. If you do not, you will re-create the problems in the future, as they are affecting the present moment.

Exercise: The letters.

Make a list of the people, living or deceased, whom you still feel you have past issues with.

Take each person individually, as you are going to write two letters to each one. The first letter must contain all the anger, guilt, jealousy, swear words, etc., and when you have exhausted all the things your mind wants to say, burn the letter. The second letter is everything you wanted to say, but without the anger, etc., and it can only include the facts. Once you have completed this letter, you have to make a decision to burn it, or send it. If you burn it, you have to let go of any emotion which is tied to the past. If you send it, you will have to be prepared for the response, and have the strength not to move from the facts. Fact is the truth, which should emerge in the second letter. Opinion, hurt, anger, etc., are the stored up emotions, which you did not express at the time, and these need to come out first, before the facts can emerge. You also have to be honest with yourself and see your part in the drama. You drew the experiences to yourself because of your first point of pain and your fears.

Once you have let the issue go, you must observe your mind in case it tries to recreate the pattern or issue. The mind thrives on conflict and for a while there will be a space where the conflict used to be. It is easy to re-fill it with other thoughts of conflict, as we are not used to a space where no thought exists.

This exercise can shift suppressed emotions within you, so allow yourself to feel them. Be aware also of any judgments you continue to hold onto after you have burnt or sent the letters. This may even cause the recipient to enter into a crisis healing of their own, but this can be the greatest gift you could give to them.

Ask yourself this question: If your mother, father, partner, child, enemy, etc., had only two minutes left to live, what would you say to them in order to show them how to solve any issues of non-love that they gave to you. If it were you who only had two minutes left to live, what would you need to hear from them, about all the non-love that you gave out?

No-one else has your distinctive thought patterns, no-one else thinks in exactly the same running commentary of words. In this sense, your egoic mind is exclusive to your conditioning and beliefs. This is what gives each person a seemingly unique personality. Underneath this egoic self is its root, which is fear.

This fear is the same for all of humanity, as it does not differentiate between one human and another. Have you ever noticed how most action movies show how the bad guys do not care about the people around them and how they use them for their own selfish gain, but the good guys are always trying to save everyone's lives and bring peace out of the chaos? This is similar to what is going on in each individual. The egoic mind does not care about your eternal being, as it cares only about its own survival. Your eternal being is always showing you the way to bring peace into your life, so do you choose to be used, or not?

Chapter 14

Purity of Thoughts, Words and Deeds

Is it possible to train the mind to have pure thoughts? This is an important question, because so many people participate on courses, or read books about positive thinking, yet the root cause of the disturbed thinking process is left untouched. It is just covered over with another batch of new words.
Purity in thought occurs when you observe your mind and no longer get caught up in any fear. Surely, if thoughts were not dictating your way of being, words and actions would be heart-based?

Your Spiritual Life

Time or gravity was created at the point of the primeval atom, and it is the space between the opposing pushing and pulling magnetic forces, so it is controlled by the mind. This is seen in the movement of the Earth from night to day, or from up to down, etc. The mind uses this process to create sequential time of the clock and calendar, but over generations, it has also become psychological time, which is the movement from one state of being to another. In order to change the state of your being, from non-enlightenment to enlightenment, you will need comparison, which creates competition. This is the whole foundation of separation between one human and another. Psychological time is therefore not love, as it is the past, which is based on fear. The desire for pleasure, whilst rejecting pain, is the coping mechanism we use to run away from this fear. If fear did not exist, would there be any desire to become anything other than what you already are?

Most people believe being spiritual is something separate from being a human, and it often has labels attached to it, which conjure up images of an austere life. If you declare yourself to be spiritual, people assume you can no longer go to a restaurant, talk about mundane things, laugh, have money, live in a nice house, etc. This meagre way of living is the egoic mind's idea of being spiritual, but the reality has nothing to do with this. To be here, fully inside your human body, which is being aware of the grosser mind-made nature of it, can be challenging, because you have to be observant of yourself in every moment. The monk who lives alone in a cave may be rigorous in observing his celibacy, but put him in a nightclub with scantily clad women and his libido will challenge him. Therefore, the real spiritual work is to be living completely immersed in human life.

The idea that celibacy is a way to God is a complete illusion. This control of a natural human function is threaded through many religious and philosophical beliefs, and many people think abstaining is crucial to receiving enlightenment. The pope, nuns, gurus, monks, lamas, priests, etc., all believe they have to 'give up' the sexual act. What exactly is this act, which is the cause of so much confusion on this planet? The act itself can have both pleasure and pain for those involved, from the depths of degradation to the heights of ecstasy. There are very few human acts, which have this within it, for instance there is no 'good' for both parties in murder, robbery or violence, but two people can have basal, animalistic sex and get pleasure out of it. The denial of sex or the overindulgence of it, are both the same thing, as underneath each one you will find desire. The priests etc., who renounce sex, desire to be God-like, while the one obsessed with sex desires the release and the fulfilment.

Procreation is a necessity for the continuation of the human species, as is food, water and air. There will always be a drive to fulfil this sexual need which arises in the human, because it is from nature, and it guarantees its survival. It may not kill you if you suppress the sexual urge, but it will affect your energy, as you will be suppressing a natural flow from within.

If you have sex in order to share love with another, then the act will have joy in it, as there is no hidden intent. Sex based on pleasure or pain, will have intent and manipulation involved, as pleasure is self-focused and pain is avoidance and denial in action.

Sex is only one of the many aspects of yourself which require vigilant self-observation, as every moment can reveal so much about you and what is actually going on within you. Have you ever really taken notice of how you do things? How you walk, speak, eat, etc? For example, you may be a fast eater, throwing food down as quickly as possible in order to move on to the next thing.   Maybe, you eat painfully slowly, holding everyone back, taking their energy and avoid taking action in life? Every little detail of what you think, say and do is revealing your egoic mind, your conditioning and your personality. None of these things is love, they are your manufactured safety zones, which you created in order to protect yourself from non-love. By living from this manufactured self, you are also giving

241

out non-love, because you are creating a wall around yourself, which is actually rejecting others, so you are giving out the very thing you are trying to avoid.

Living a spiritual life is therefore living a whole life. This includes what is going on internally and externally. To focus only on one aspect will bring about an imbalance. For example, people who do various external pursuits such as yoga, tai chi meditation, healing or sports, may appear to be physically well and fit, but internally they can be in chaos. To be spiritual is to have harmony between the internal and the external life.

The Majority of Humans do not Know What They Do

Most people are not consciously aware of their thoughts and their emotional reactions, and they have very little or only a basic understanding of the inner work. Even though they may have a magnitude of so-called spiritual knowledge, they still do not know how they are affecting themselves, others and the world. For example, the pope may have to participate in various acts of worship, prayers, ablutions, and confessions throughout his daily life, but in the long run he is keeping millions of people in illusion. If you took him out of his world, dressed him in jeans and a t-shirt, and put him in the middle of Delhi in India, the shock would be huge. His current life is evidently based on a very careful programme of tasks and rituals concerning mind-made beliefs, and many people around him see to his needs and ensure this way of living continues. His world is therefore actually small and isolated, because it is only based on the mind, and as the external reflects the internal, the internal will also be just as small and isolated.

Another example of this small way of living is of the monk who lived in a monastery in Ireland. After staying here for more than a decade he decided to leave, so exchanging his robes for normal everyday clothes, he left for the city of Dublin. The city was not a strange place to him, as he had visited it regularly as a monk, but within ten minutes of walking down the main high street he went into a state of shock. People were blindly walking at him, bumping into him and cursing at him and he did not understand why, and he became angry. It was only later, upon reflection that he realised what the problem was. For the last ten years he had walked down this very same high street in his monk's habit, and people had moved out of his way and made a special passage for him to pass through. They had deemed him something spiritual and different from them, but now, as a normal man, without the monk image, he was like the rest of them and the special treatment had ended.

When you begin to look within yourself you will find there is a sense of frustration or anger. Sometimes you direct this at other people, and sometimes at yourself. If you look closer at this, you will see how you expect others to prove they love you by fulfilling certain roles, or you expect them to be able to mind-read your requests and know what needs to be done. If they do not do things which bring you pleasure, it confirms your belief system that they do not love you.

The opposite to this pleasure is any pain you have experienced as a result of another person's actions and perhaps this has brought you anger and frustration at not being able to get justice, or maybe you cannot explain why certain things have happened to you which have brought you suffering. All these things need to be looked at, because your reactions to circumstances are what keep the anger within you active.

Exercise: List the names of all the main people in your life.

1. Under each name, write down all the things you expect from them.
2. If they do not do them, do you get angry, frustrated, or do you reject them?
3. Can you look at this anger within you?
4. If you trace it back, what belief is it attached to?
5. If you were to look at that belief, would you say it was due to not being loved?
6. Can you feel this deep rooted sense of rejection?

243

Can you now look at each person on your list and see that between them, they are the whole of your past? Can you look at all the times you have been angry and frustrated, or rejected them, as they did not give you love in the way you believe they should have done?

When an upsetting event occurs, for example, someone steals your car and you feel angry, is this upset actually anger, or is it a state of shock because the act from another person is not love? Does anger occur after the shock? What is this anger? It is an energy which follows thought, so your mind is upset because you were not protected and out pour all the thoughts. This is your first point of pain happening all over again. There is no difference. Solve your first point of pain, which heals the reactions and you will deal with life circumstances in awareness of the anger, and you will be able to observe and feel at the same time.

If you have gone into this without your mind analysing and judging, life will never be the same again, because you will have reached a deep understanding about the state of humanity. You will know without a doubt that people are not aware of what they are doing, because they are all living from this state of trying to get love according to what they believe love is. Each human has their own unique conditioning, so the rules will be different and changeable.

The anger, which is set up from your first point of pain has two points from which it works, revenge and proving you don't need love. The revenge types will want justice or the same suffering to occur to those who caused them to suffer, and those who try to prove themselves will reject non-love with a 'I'll show them' attitude. Both types are angry. Some are more explosive, whilst others are quietly seething. Neither is consciously aware of what is really going on within. Every human has this within them. Even those who would deny it and are externally passive and quiet, have this anger within them. It is the closest emotion to fear.

Some people think karma means correcting the acts of non-love you did in a past life, by acting with love in this life, but acts of kindness do not necessarily end the effect of non-love, as you may be acting out of an expectation of yourself. For example, a woman takes an oath not to kill any living thing, but one day a mosquito lands on her baby, she tries to gently shoo it off without harming it, or putting any stress into the air, but it bites the child and infects her with malaria. Consequently, the baby dies, and now the woman is angry. For the anger to occur, it must have already been there, probably sitting very quietly under the oath of being kind to everything, waiting until it was provoked. Originally, the woman did not need to take the oath, she just had to look at the anger.

If there is such a thing as reincarnation and karma, then this very act of getting to the root of this anger will end the karmic packages, because revenge and striving will cease, as will any expectations of others and yourself. In its place understanding and compassion emerge. Not the type that says, 'I am on a higher level because others can't see or know what I can.' This is condescending, and you have not really observed the anger. A true understanding is very clear, as you are totally aware of the illusion in another and you realise it is because they fear receiving non-love.

The End of All Authority

If you have read the words in this book without judging them, analysing them, or rejecting them, you should have come across this extraordinary feeling of being completely alone. All the external and internal authority will have revealed itself. The external authority being all those people you have given your personal power to and the internal authority being all those voices in your mind, which are fighting for your attention with all of their beliefs of 'you should' and 'you should not'. Your eternal being, which communicates to you through the inner voice based on feelings and facts, has to be the governor of your own life, as there is no-one else internally or externally who can save you, free you, or show you the vast eternal being of who you are. Only you can go inside of you, and sift through all the illusion to find this priceless gem.

No guru, priest, lama, Buddhist or abbot can take you to this divine place. They cannot even help you, because they are caught in a role and an image. If a person goes within, whilst still holding on to any external belief, system, teaching or path, they will be challenged to let it go, as the folly and limitation of the belief will reveal itself. Many people get stuck at this point, because they do want not let go of things which have brought them power over others, or comfort. They refuse to look at the madness of the belief, and they reject or avoid the way out of the illusion. There can be no judgment, just the awareness.

This relinquishing of authority is not the dissolution of it, for example, a certain amount of external authority is required in order to learn a subject or a skill. The relinquishing of authority referred to is meant in the terms of unnecessary external and psychological authority: looking to another to solve your problems, or guide you to some imaginary deity. To put an end to this psychological authority you would need to listen for the guidance of the inner voice and end all the opinions, judgments and the striving to become. Only then can the moment present itself as 'new', because the past is no longer infiltrating it, and the future is not moving into a safe zone in order to keep fearful events of the past from re-occurring. A life without unnecessary external and psychological authority gives you the freedom to discover, as all the opposites of 'right' and 'wrong' have ended, therefore the egoic mind is no longer in control of your human life, 'you' are.

This life is important. *You* are important. It does not matter about any supposed past lives, or proposed future lives, as this is the mind enquiring into the unknown in order to make it known, so that it can use any information it finds. What really counts is how you live this life. Do you live it from your inner voice, which is your eternal being, or do you live it from the mind with its opposites? This is all you have to ask yourself in every moment.

Part Four Summary

Where are You Now?

Your life purpose is to be fully present in every moment. This includes being completely aware of, and acting upon, your diet, health, home, environment, work, relationships, emotions, thoughts, etc. Any excuse not to be living a whole life will come from your mind, so is the passion strong enough? Do you want to get inside of you and bring the distortion back into a state of love? There is no other life purpose. We might like to believe that material success, or teaching the masses some form of religious or spiritual discipline, is valuable, but it is only mind-based, and there is nothing permanent within it. Love is permanent, so would it not be better for you to only look at this one thing, to give your whole attention to it, your passion and your life? If not, what else is there to do?

Purity of thoughts, words and deeds are paramount to your life and to the life of every material thing, as all this came from the one seed of the primeval atom, which gives you the ability to affect everything. To immerse yourself in wholeness, or in this vast space of love, you have to recognise what is not love in you. Is your anger, frustration, jealousy, desire, etc., love? Or, because of your conditioning, have you accepted non-love as a way of living, thinking everyone else does it so why not you? Very few people stop and question the basis of their life. Most people accept the distortion and they call it 'normal', simply because they do not know there is another way to live.

You are now at your very own cross-roads. If you read this book with just your mind and did not put any realisations into action, or complete the exercises, you will probably put the essence of this book aside and continue in your old patterns. If you have realised the truth, are you now afraid of the changes this truth may bring into your life?

Whether or not you decide to have a relationship with your inner voice, and ultimately your eternal self, or you reject all that has been written, you can never go back to not knowing, and any excuse you give to yourself will cause you to be uncomfortable. At the end of your life, you cannot say, 'I did not know', because you did. The eternal in you knows everything, and now you know there is a connection with it inside of you. If you walk the journey of your life with it, all that is not love within you will have to be revealed and torn down. If you walk away, you have to know and accept that your mind is in control and your life purpose will amount to nothing permanent.

You know who you are
You know what it is all about
You know your life purpose

You are eternal, and you chose to come here to bring love into nature, and you naturally give love and receive love, transmuting everything you sense, think, say and do into love. Is there a better way to live?

Upon Reflection

The Answer is Always in the Question

The question, 'What does the world need right now?', was asked at the beginning of this book. Whatever your answer was; peace, love, honesty, etc., is the precise opposite of what is actually occurring. The human is in a state of chaos, and therefore the world is in a state of chaos. You are the world and the world is you.

Humanity is one whole material essence made up from billions of human forms, which are the fragments that make a whole, but if the fragments resist and remain apart from each other, then the whole cannot be formed. As long as there is this sense of separation, humanity will work for the betterment of each fragment, and this is a self-centred egoic activity.

At the foundation of humanity, we find this root of fear, which leads to anger, desire, jealousy, envy, etc. Every human has this root, and fundamentally, we are no different from each other. Individual conditioning and world history are what keep us believing we are separate entities, because if you strip away all of your conditioning, your fears, your anger, your judgments and opinions, you will find you are not separate from anyone else. Separation is the great illusion.

There are two voices within you, the inner voice and the egoic mind. Humanity as a whole is only listening to the inner voice approximately ten per cent of the time. The rest of the time we are listening to the egoic mind, which thrives on opposites, competition, comparison and confusion. The egoic mind is the sustaining force behind war, murder, theft, poverty, starvation, disease, karma and even death. It governs all material life including humans, animals, nature and the cosmos. It has no place beyond the mind, because it is the mind, and therefore it cannot go beyond itself.

If we are to bring peace to this world and end all of the chaos, we need to begin with ourselves. We need to find out how the egoic mind is working in us, so that we can understand it and end its games of chaos and separation. The truth is: it is not what the world needs right now, it is what you need right now, because you are the same thing. Solve it in you, and you will solve it in the world, because as you apply this solution to your life, you will shift humanity as a whole into listening more to the inner voice, which is love.

You do not need an external teacher, because your inner voice is your teacher. All you need to do is listen within and take the necessary action, but many people claim to know the way, or have 'special' knowledge. Another person can only show you the depth of you, if they have gone to the depth of themselves, and when you see yourself for who you are, you see this other person is also 'you'. This is not a mental concept, it is real, it is liberating and it is the end of all chaos. Any authority also ends, and sharing takes its place. The eternal 'you', expressed through another person, will only *ever* lead you back inside to your real self.

The slayer of love is the egoic mind, and it will lead you to strive for some form of deity, image or concept of yourself, which is not real. There is no external God, as the love of the Beloved lives in you. Your inner voice is your very own personal connection to love and your eternal being *is* love. When you are following this voice, you have given the human form over for the expression of this love, in fact, you have become love and you are acting, speaking, and living with love. This is what you came here to do. To do anything else will bring you suffering.

The Mirror

You are on a battlefield fighting with another warrior, yet every step you take, the opposing warrior mirrors your movement. No matter how you try to defeat him, he matches your expertise and he is as quick and as strong as you are. As this realisation sinks in, you begin to observe the warrior, and you deliberately make mistakes and take risks to see what he will do, but still he copies your movements. Eventually, you begin to wonder what would happen if you lowered your sword, so you take the gamble and to your surprise the warrior does the same. You stare at each other before turning to look around you; all the other warriors on the battlefield have also dropped their swords.

Feeling tired and despondent, you decide that enough is enough, and it is time to end this war. From your observations, you decide to test the realisation that the warrior will mirror you, so you turn your back on him and walk away, and you smile to yourself when he does the same. The war has ended and you have surrendered by walking away, but you also realise you could easily re-start the battle, as all along you have been fighting your very own inexhaustible shadow. There can be no winner in this fight, only surrender.

Your very first experience of non-love will have created the belief that love is not strong enough to protect you and guide you through this battlefield of material living, so you have created a shadow version of yourself. The true spiritual essence of your real self was put away in a box for safe-keeping and you became a slave to the mind.

Love is stronger than the mind, as it is vast and limitless, and the mind is small, alone and limited. Living a material life is similar to going into the home of the mind, but you are only a visitor, yet you believe you live there. It is time to put down the games of the mind, bid your host farewell, open the door and step out into the sunshine. When you look back at the home of mind, you will see it for what it really is, and you will wonder how your vast eternal self got trapped into such a small space. Therefore, let this book be a mirror, so that you can clearly see this shadow of yourself and drop the conditioning which has trapped you. Feel your true essence, surrender to it, and be who you really are.

You are not Alone because You are All-one

In that place deep inside,
You believe you are alone,
The egoic mind *is* alone,
And this brings individual and world chaos,
When you truly go into the vast emptiness and loneliness,
You will find how the empty space is not empty at all,
It is actually full,
Of you...
The egoic mind does not know what is in this space,
So, it labels it as empty or lonely,
What is in this space cannot be described,
It can be felt,
Silently communicated with,
And if you listen carefully,
It will speak back to you...

If you change anything in your life today, let it be the turning within, the observation of the mind and the listening for the inner voice of love.

Mike Robinson.

About the Author

Mike Robinson has travelled the world teaching on the topic of the real self and the illusions which keep a person trapped in their suffering. Mike only ever helps a person to look at the fact of a situation, which is the truth, and truth has no sides, no judgment and no 'right' or 'wrong', it is 'as it is' and therefore it is love in action.

There is an ease and grace that flows out of this gentle man who has touched thousands of lives. No-one leaves Mike's presence unaffected by the unshakeable peace and truth that emanates from his being.

For more information visit his website:
www.mikerobinson.eu.com